NATIONAL TRUST

Book of
Crumbles

NATIONAL TRUST

Book of
Crumbles

Laura Mason

National Trust

First published in the United Kingdom in 2018 by
National Trust Books
43 Great Ormond Street
London
WC1N 3HZ

An imprint of Pavilion Books Group Ltd

Volume © National Trust Books, 2018
Text © Laura Mason, 2018
Illustrations by Louise Morgan, 2018

ISBN: 9781911358473

A CIP catalogue record for this book is available from the British Library.

10 9 8 7 6 5 4 3 2

Reproduction by Rival Colour Ltd, UK
Printed and bound by GPS Group, Slovenia

This book can be ordered direct from the publisher at the website:
www.pavilionbooks.com, or try your local bookshop. Also available at
National Trust shops or www.nationaltrustbooks.co.uk

Contents

Introduction   6

Fruit Crumbles   8

Fruit Cobblers   28

Crumble Tarts and Cakes   44

Crumble Muffins and Slices   68

Savoury Crumbles   88

Savoury Cobblers   102

Creative Crumbles   118

Notes   139

Index   140

Acknowledgements   143

Introduction

Crumbles and cobblers hold a special place in all our hearts. They are rustic dishes, generous in spirit, informal and quickly put together. The sweet versions rely on a combination of storecupboard ingredients and seasonally plentiful and cheap fruit, or fruit from a freezer or tin. Ideal for cooks in a hurry, the quantities easily multiply up to feed a family plus an unexpected guest or two; these are hospitable, big-hearted dishes that can be put in the oven and left to cook.

The smell of a fruit crumble baking is pudding heaven, with toasty notes of browning butter, sugar and warm fruit. Crumbles are dishes for all seasons, good-tempered, adaptable and easily improvised. They lighten leaden grey days and bolster one against chilly and blustery weather. In a berry crumble, the perfume of hot, jammy fruit can even enhance a warm summer day. As food writer Nigel Slater – someone whose affection for crumbles shines off the page – says, they are comfort food of the first order. Everyone has their favourite bits: the crisp surface, or the edge where the juice has boiled up and caramelised the crumb. And they are nearly as good cold the next day.

Cobblers share many of the characteristics of crumbles, but the patchwork topping of a classic cobbler is described in North America (the home of these dishes) as biscuit dough. This means soft biscuits, akin to scones or dumplings, as they are known in Britain. Often containing relatively little fat and sugar, and bound with milk or buttermilk, they can be somewhat less calorific than crumbles. The crunch comes from the baked outer edge; the centre is softer. However, puddings in the cobbler category vary in texture from nearly a cake to almost a pie. A sweet cobbler made with buttermilk or sour cream biscuit dough and peaches or berries is a composition in which simple ingredients become a sumptuous pudding which everyone loves.

Although we tend to think of them as sweet, both crumbles and cobblers make good savoury dishes. Leave out the sugar, flavour the toppings with cheese or herbs, and use a filling of meat, fish or vegetables in a well-seasoned sauce to give a satisfying family dinner. These are essentially stews with a topping. They are more rustic than gratins, easier to make than pies, and share the attributes of homely comfort food exhibited by their sweet cousins. A few quickly cooked vegetables or a salad complete the meal.

Crumble topping can also be a star in its own right. A sweet crumb mixture, spiced or otherwise, enhances many favourite North American breakfast and brunch cakes, and provides a crisp topping for fruit pies. Baked alone, the buttery crumbs add crunch when sprinkled over cooked fruit or creamy desserts, the principle behind the deconstructed crumble, in which each element is prepared separately. Originally a phenomenon of restaurant cooking, this is the solution for anyone who disagrees that the soggy bit where the crust and fruit have been in contact during cooking is actually the best part of a crumble. Both crumbles and cobblers are brilliant puddings for novice cooks and children to practice their culinary skills on. Gather a basket of apples or berries and a few other simple ingredients, and get crumbling.

Fruit Crumbles

Never-fail Apple Crumble

A simple recipe. The crumble topping is really easy to make and always pleases.

About 1kg Bramley apples
100g granulated sugar
Finely grated zest and juice of 1
    lemon

FOR THE TOPPING
220g plain flour
110g granulated sugar
110g butter, cut into cubes

Preheat the oven to 180°C.

Peel and core the apples and roughly chop the flesh. Put the chopped apples into a baking dish, together with the sugar, lemon zest and juice. Cover with foil and bake for 20–30 minutes or until the apple is starting to soften. Remove and leave to cool a little.

For the topping, mix the flour and sugar together and rub in the butter until the mixture resembles fine breadcrumbs. Tip the mixture over the apple. Put the dish on an oven tray and return to the oven for 30–40 minutes or until the top is pale gold and developing cracks and the juice is starting to bubble up round the edges. Serve warm with custard, cream or ice cream.

Good Companions: Crumble Fillings

With apples, try a little ground cinnamon instead of lemon. Cloves are traditional, but not everyone likes them: use ground cloves sparingly, along with a little ground cinnamon. Add a handful of sultanas for extra sweetness, if you like their texture.

Pears make good crumbles; for added flavour, try cinnamon, a few slices of stem ginger or a little vanilla essence. Half apple and half pear is also good. Both apples and pears can be cooked in a little water or juice before the topping is added; this is partly down to personal preference, and if you're a bit short of time you can put them in the oven in the baking dish while you prepare the crumble topping.

Autumn brings blackberries: use them alone, tossed with a little sugar and cornflour, or try half blackberry and half apple for a classic British combination.

Rhubarb is an excellent crumble filling, both the early forced rhubarb or the outdoor rhubarb from later in the year; flavour with orange zest and juice. Gooseberries are another classic crumble fruit. Vanilla sugar is good for sweetening both rhubarb and gooseberries; use it generously as they are acidic fruit.

Plums of any kind make lovely crumbles. Cinnamon, cardamom or vanilla go well with these, as do almondy flavours: add a drop of almond essence or a couple of crumbled amaretti biscuits to the fruit, or crack a few plum stones and put the kernels in the filling (do note that plum kernels should never be eaten raw). Other stone fruit, such as peaches and apricots, are also excellent crumble material.

Prepare fruit by peeling, coring and stoning as necessary (although small plums such as damsons are difficult and sometimes it's best just to leave the stones in – though be cautious when feeding young children). Cut into bite-sized pieces and add a little water, lemon or orange juice to help the initial cooking.

Apple Crisp

There is no clear distinction between a crumble and a crisp, but the latter name is often used when the topping includes oats. Cooking it relatively slowly gives a toasted, nutty flavour. Good with apples, pears, plums, peaches or apricots and the simple flavours of lemon or orange.

600–700g Bramley apples, peeled and cored
Finely grated zest and juice of 1 lemon (preferably unwaxed)
20–30g soft pale brown sugar

FOR THE TOPPING
120g plain flour
60g porridge oats
90g soft pale brown sugar
Pinch of salt
90g butter, cut into cubes

Preheat the oven to 160°C.

Cut the apple into small chunks (1–1.5cm) and pile into a baking dish. Pour over the lemon juice and add about 4 tablespoons water. Scatter in the lemon zest and the sugar.

To make the topping, mix the flour, oats, sugar and salt. Rub in the butter to make a slightly lumpy mixture. Crumble this over the apples. Put the dish on an oven tray and bake for about 1 hour or until the fruit is soft and the topping crisp.

Leave to cool a little before serving. This dish is good with custard or thick cream.

Rhubarb and Strawberry Crumble

Rhubarb and strawberries go well together. Forced pink rhubarb is delicate and pretty, but expensive. Outdoor rhubarb is more robust and cheaper (or free if there's some in the garden). Choose rhubarb with slender stems.

About 300g rhubarb (trimmed weight), washed

About 200g strawberries, hulled and washed

40–60g caster sugar

FOR THE TOPPING

90g butter

Seeds scraped from ½ a vanilla pod

180g plain flour

90g caster sugar

Pinch of salt

Preheat the oven to 170°C.

Cut the rhubarb into 1cm lengths (if the stems are thick, cut them in half lengthways first) and put it into a baking dish. Halve or quarter the strawberries and scatter over the rhubarb. Add sugar to taste.

To make the topping, melt the butter in a small pan and heat until it froths and turns slightly brown, with a nutty smell. Immediately remove from the heat and add the vanilla. Leave to cool a little.

Mix the flour, sugar and a tiny pinch of salt, then pour in the butter, stirring constantly, to form a crumbly mixture. Spoon this over the fruit.

Put the dish on an oven tray and bake for about 40 minutes, or until the top is golden and the juice is bubbling up round the sides.

Leave to cool a little before serving. Clotted cream or a Proper Egg Custard (page 135) are good with this.

Raspberry Gingerbread Crumble

The topping for this is based on the short-textured gingerbread that has been made in Grasmere in the Lake District since the nineteenth century.

About 500g fresh raspberries
150g butter, cut into cubes
250g self-raising flour
to

120g soft pale brown sugar
1 teaspoon ground ginger
½ teaspoon finely grated lemon zest

Preheat the oven to 180°C.

Put the raspberries into a baking dish. Rub the butter into the flour, then stir in the sugar, ginger and lemon zest. Sprinkle the mixture over the fruit, but don't press it down.

Put the dish on an oven tray and bake for 30 minutes. Serve warm with thick cream.

Sweet Crumble Toppings

If in doubt, stick to the proportions of two parts plain flour, one part sugar and one part butter (Never-fail Crumble, page 10). Slightly higher proportions of sugar and butter make for crisper results.

White wheat flour is the usual choice for crumbles. For variety, try replacing some of the flour with ground almonds, porridge oats or crumbled crisp amaretti, stirred in after the butter is rubbed in. Wholemeal flour makes a heavy topping.

Using partially refined sugars adds subtle caramelised flavours: try golden granulated or golden caster sugar, demerara, or a proportion of soft pale brown sugar, but nothing darker. A tiny pinch of salt in the mixture, especially if using unsalted butter, is an enhancement. Ground ginger or cinnamon are worth trying as spices for the topping. Vanilla is a lovely flavour as well: use vanilla sugar for just a whisper, or a little vanilla essence or paste mixed into melted butter for something more assertive.

The traditional way to make crumble is to rub the butter into the flour and sugar using your fingertips, to give a breadcrumb-like texture. Or you can pulse the mixture in a food processor to give a crumbly texture. Alternatively, melt the butter, let it cool and stir it into the flour and sugar – a simple method that produces a less powdery texture. Browning the butter adds a nutty note to a plain crumble mixture.

A scattering of flaked almonds or chopped pistachios over the top is a nice finish, particularly good with stone fruit; or try chopped hazelnuts for pears.

Liquid isn't usually added to crumble mixtures, although the food writer Nigel Slater suggests sprinkling a tablespoon of water into a standard mix and combining it roughly with a fork, to give a lumpy rather than a powdery mixture. When baked, this gives a variegated texture with crisp little nuggets among the crumble. Egg is an unusual ingredient in crumble mixes, but it is sometimes added to bind Central European streusel and richer pastry-type mixes. Finally, to enhance the appearance of crumble-topped cakes and muffins, add a dusting of powdered sugar or a drizzle of icing.

Apple Brown Betty

This apple pudding uses breadcrumbs for crunch. Make your own the old-fashioned way, by drying stale white bread (not sourdough) in a low oven and crushing it with a rolling pin. The pudding is made in a deep mould, such as a soufflé dish or deep cake tin.

5–6 tart eating apples (about 700g)
60g butter, plus extra for greasing
150g dry breadcrumbs
½ teaspoon ground cinnamon
½ teaspoon ground cloves

½ teaspoon grated nutmeg
120g soft pale brown sugar
Grated zest and juice of 1 lemon
   (preferably unwaxed)

Preheat the oven to 180°C.

Generously butter a 15–16 cm diameter soufflé dish or a deep cake tin with a fixed base.

Peel, quarter and core the apples, then cut them widthways into small thin slices. Melt the butter and stir three quarters of it into the breadcrumbs. Mix the spices with the sugar.

Spread a third of the buttered crumbs over the base of the dish or tin. Put half of the apples on top of this, sprinkling them with lemon juice and half of the zest and pressing them down firmly (packing the mixture down is part of the secret of this pudding). Spoon half of the sugar and spice mix over, pressing it down with the back of a spoon. Add another third of the buttered crumbs, then the remaining apples, the remaining lemon zest and some more lemon juice. Pack the rest of the spiced sugar over the top and finish with the rest of the crumbs, pressing everything down well. The volume will shrink during cooking. Pour over any remaining lemon juice and splash with the remaining butter. Cover the top with a baking paper or a well buttered piece of foil.

Bake for 25 minutes, then uncover and bake for a further 30–40 minutes, or until the apple is soft.

Leave to cool a little before serving with cream or ice cream.

Crumble Variations: Bettys

A betty is an American dessert that is not strictly a crumble or a cobbler, but is easily put together and has a crunchy texture derived from dry breadcrumbs mixed with butter, and layered with spiced apple. The origins are obscure but it has been made in North America since the mid-nineteenth century. A comforting dish when well made, it has many European relatives. In early twentieth-century English cookery books, bread and apple puddings were sometimes called Swiss apple cake, apple charlotte, or simply baked apple pudding.

Apricot and Pistachio Crumble

Apricots, pistachios and flower waters were all fashionable ingredients for puddings in large eighteenth-century houses, even if crumble was unknown. This can be baked in individual ramekins for a more elegant dessert.

About 800g fresh apricots, stoned and cut into small pieces

30g caster sugar, or to taste

1 teaspoon orange flower water or rose water (optional)

FOR THE TOPPING

60g unsalted pistachios

120g self-raising flour

60g caster sugar

Pinch of salt

60g butter, cut into cubes

Preheat the oven to 170°C.

Put the apricots into a baking dish and sprinkle over the caster sugar and orange flower or rose water.

For the topping, roughly chop the pistachios – best done with a knife, rather than a food processor – and set aside. Mix the flour, sugar and salt, add the butter and rub in, or pulse in a food processor, until the mixture resembles fine breadcrumbs. Stir the pistachios through the mix, then use it to cover the fruit.

Put the dish on an oven tray and bake for 35–45 minutes, or until the top is pale gold and the fruit is soft. Don't let it brown: if this starts to happen, turn down the heat and cook a little longer. Serve warm with thick cream or vanilla ice cream.

Plum and Amaretti Crumble

Quite sweet but relatively light on the butter, this uses amaretti biscuits for texture and an intense almond note. In late summer, try it with the rich but acidic flesh of damsons, whose spring blossom is such a feature of the Lyth Valley near Sizergh Castle in Cumbria.

600–700g plums, damsons, nectarines or peaches
Caster sugar, to taste
FOR THE TOPPING
60g plain flour
60g crisp amaretti biscuits, crushed

60g golden caster sugar (or granulated sugar)
60g ground almonds
30g butter, melted and cooled but still liquid
30g flaked almonds

Preheat the oven to 180°C.

If using plums, peaches or nectarines, stone them and cut into quarters or eighths. Damsons are small and squashy: leave the stones in, but warn your guests. Put the fruit in a baking dish and add sugar if you think it is under-ripe or acidic. Damsons are most in need of it, but don't overdo it.

To make the topping, mix the flour, crushed biscuits, sugar and ground almonds. Drizzle in the melted butter, stirring to make a crumbly texture. Spread this over the fruit. Scatter the flaked almonds on top.

Put the dish on an oven tray and bake for 25–30 minutes or until the top is golden brown and the juices are bubbling through. Keep an eye on it and if the almonds are browning too quickly, turn down the heat and cook a little longer. Serve warm with thick cream or ice cream.

Containers and Cooking Tips

Almost all mid-twentieth-century British households owned an oval stoneware baking dish with sloping sides, used for everything from stewing fruit in the oven to making pies. The traditional cream or dark treacly brown colours and smooth surfaces of the dish were homely contrasts to the pale golds and rough textures of crumble toppings. Ovenproof glass in the form of Pyrex must have been such a novelty, allowing sight of the fillings and their contrasting colours.

Ovenproof ceramic or glass containers are still best for cooking crumble. The pudding is served straight from the baking dish, so if shopping try to find a nice one. Any reasonably well-equipped kitchen should have a dish suitable for holding a crumble that will serve four to six people, and there are lots available in homeware shops. One around 18 x 20 x 7.5cm will hold a crumble that feeds four people generously; the capacity will be around 1.2 to 1.5 litres. Depth is perhaps most important: 7–7.5cm seems ideal, allowing for roughly two thirds fruit to one third crumble in the finished product, although a couple of centimetres shallower will still produce a good result. Although crumbles are generally for sharing, large ramekins can be used to bake individual portions.

The proportion of sweet filling to crumble is partly down to personal taste. Lots of crumble, and the fruit will seem on the thin side. Not so much, and the topping becomes a meagre handful on an ocean of juice. Experienced cooks estimate by eye, mentally balancing the size of the dish against the number of diners, doing a quick sum relating to topping ingredients. Bear in mind that the fruit (especially apples) will collapse as cooking progresses. Compensate for this by heaping the filling high in the middle.

When baking, always put the crumble dish on an oven tray to catch spills as it cooks. Hot fruit and sugar can be unpredictable and messy. If the crumble seems to be browning too fast (especially if it has chopped nuts on top), turn the heat down and cook for a little longer. Slow cooking can actually enhance the texture of the fruit filling and help crisp up the buttery, sugary crumble.

Serving temperature is a matter of personal choice, but the optimum seems to be when the fruit has cooled slightly and the toasty flavours of the topping are most apparent.

Made too much topping? Find another dish and make an extra crumble. No one will complain. Alternatively, put the mixture in a ziplock bag and store in the freezer for up to two months. Use it straight from the bag over fresh fruit. The cooking time shouldn't be much longer than that for a crumble using freshly made topping.

Pre-prepared crumbles can also be frozen and go straight from freezer to oven for cooking. For uncooked ones, as a general rule, cover with foil and bake at 180°C for 90 minutes, then turn the heat up to 220°C and continue to bake until the filling is bubbling. Remove the foil for the last few minutes to brown the surface. Frozen but fully cooked crumble can also go straight to the oven. Heat on 180°C until thoroughly hot all the way through.

Quince, Pear and Apple Crumble with Marzipan

Full of golden autumn flavours, this a special crumble for a grey chilly day. Quinces need long preliminary cooking to soften them before the rest of the fruit is added.

500–600g quinces

150g granulated sugar

1 piece star anise

About 400g apples – a firm eating
    variety such as Cox's

About 400g pears, such as Conference

FOR THE TOPPING

120g plain flour

30g demerara sugar

50g butter

60g marzipan, cut into small chunks

1–2 tablespoons flaked almonds

Preheat the oven to 180°C.

Peel the quinces (use a potato peeler), cut them into quarters and remove the cores, then cut each quarter lengthways into two or three thin slices. Put them in a large baking dish with the granulated sugar, the star anise and about 150ml water. Cover and bake for 1–1½ hours. Stir and cook uncovered for a further 30 minutes: the fruit should soften and turn a pinky-gold colour.

Peel, quarter and core the apples. Cut each piece in slices lengthways. Add to the quinces, cover, and bake for a further 30 minutes. If the pears are hard and unripe, peel, core and slice and add at this stage as well: otherwise, they can be added just before the crumble topping.

To make the topping, mix the flour and sugar. Put the butter and marzipan in a pan and heat gently, stirring all the time, until the marzipan has melted. Don't let it get too hot. Pour this into the flour mixture, stirring with a fork, to form a breadcrumb-like texture.

Distribute the topping mixture over the fruit. Scatter the flaked almonds over. Put the dish on an oven tray and bake for 30–40 minutes, until the topping is golden brown.

Good on its own, or serve with a little mascarpone or vanilla ice cream.

Quinces

Quinces were held in high esteem in the past; many large houses would have grown them in the sixteenth, seventeenth and eighteenth centuries. Some National Trust gardens have examples of this slightly magical tree. There is one at Coughton Court (Warwickshire), whose Tudor inhabitants no doubt enjoyed quince pastes. Moseley Old Hall (Staffordshire), a house with Elizabethan origins, has another. Visit in the autumn, preferably on a sunny day: when the fruit is ripe it perfumes the air around them. Quinces also grow at Sizergh (Cumbria), Wimpole (Cambridgeshire) and Red House at Bexleyheath on the outskirts of London, a lovely example of Arts and Crafts architecture, co-designed by William Morris.

In recognition of the Elizabethan origins of Lyveden (Northamptonshire), the orchard there includes quinces. Lyveden's wider collection of fruit trees contains historic varieties of apple, pear and plums flanking an avenue of walnuts. These have all been chosen with reference to a letter of 1597 in which Sir Thomas Tresham, the original owner of the estate, recorded his interest in planting an orchard of many fruit trees. The current project aims to restore the orchard close to the sixteenth-century original.

The sweetly scented golden fruit is rock-hard but full of pectin. Marmalade (from *marmelo*, the Portuguese word for quince) was originally a sweet, solid paste of quince and sugar, similar to Spanish *membrillo*. Noble ladies valued the fruit highly and loved the colour change, from vaguely pink to a deep, rusty red, that slow cooking brings about in the fruit.

Quinces are gorgeous in crumbles, but need much longer cooking than apples and pears. They combine well with these fruit and benefit from additional flavourings such as rose water (the historic choice) or star anise (a more contemporary one).

Fruit Cobblers

Apple and Blackberry Cobbler

Cobblers work best with fruit that produces lots of juice, as in this quintessential British fruit combination.

400–500g Bramley apples, peeled
   and cored
About 300g blackberries
75g granulated sugar
Pinch of ground cloves
Juice of 1 lemon
1 tablespoon cornflour

FOR THE TOPPING
150g plain flour, plus extra for dusting
50g granulated sugar, plus extra for
   topping (optional)
2 teaspoons baking powder
¼ teaspoon bicarbonate of soda
60g butter, melted and cooled but
   still liquid
80ml buttermilk

Preheat the oven to 190°C.

Cut the apples into thin slices and put into a bowl with the blackberries, sugar, cloves, lemon juice and cornflour. Mix well and tip into the baking dish in which you intend to cook the cobbler. Cover with foil, put the dish on an oven tray and bake for 25 minutes.

Towards the end of the cooking time, make the topping. Mix the flour, sugar, baking powder and bicarbonate of soda together. Just before the fruit is cooked, stir in the melted butter and buttermilk to make a very soft dough. Dust a work surface with flour and turn the mixture onto it. Cut into eight pieces and quickly shape these into rough discs.

Remove the fruit mixture from the oven, discard the foil and place the pieces of dough on top. Scatter another 1–2 tablespoons of sugar over the top if liked. Return to the oven on the tray for 25 minutes. Serve warm with sour cream or ice cream.

Fresh Peach Cobbler

A classic dish of southern USA cookery. You can use drained, tinned peaches if fresh aren't available.

8 large fresh peaches (or 800g tinned peaches, drained)
60g granulated sugar
Juice of 1 lemon
A few drops vanilla essence
2 teaspoons cornflour

FOR THE TOPPING
175g plain flour
150g golden caster or soft pale brown sugar
½ teaspoon salt
100g butter, cut into small cubes
75ml boiling water
1–2 tablespoons demerara sugar

Preheat the oven to 200°C.

Place the peaches into a pan of boiling water for 15 seconds, then drain and peel off the skins. Cut the fruit in half, discard the stones, and then cut each half into four slices. Mix them with the granulated sugar, lemon juice, vanilla essence and cornflour. Tip into a baking dish, cover with foil, place on an oven tray and bake for 10 minutes.

To make the topping, mix the flour, sugar and salt. Add the butter and rub in, or pulse in a food processor, until the mixture resembles breadcrumbs. Set aside.

Remove the peaches from the oven. Add the boiling water to the topping mix and stir just enough to make a dough. Distribute this in spoonfuls over the hot fruit (no need to spread it or attempt to neaten the top). Scatter a tablespoon or two of demerara sugar over and return to the oven on the oven tray for 30 minutes, until the top is golden and crisp and the filling bubbling around the edges.

Leave to cool for a few minutes before serving with vanilla ice cream.

Making Sweet Cobblers

The best known cobbler topping is based on American soft biscuits, which to British tastes are similar to plain scones, well risen, with just a hint of sweetness. Variety comes from the fats and liquids used for mixing. Buttermilk is a traditional choice for a light, fluffy result. Sour cream is an especially nice topping for berries, giving a subtle buttery tang. Milk and egg can be used if nothing else is available. A scattering of demerara sugar over the top before it goes into the oven adds crunch.

Peach cobbler is one of the best-known recipes, associated with the south-eastern USA where peaches grow well. Blueberries, which grow wild in places along the north-eastern seaboard of North America, are another traditional cobbler filling. Mixtures of fruit work well, and don't be snobby about using canned or frozen fruit: nineteenth-century immigrants to North America would have relied on preserved fruit in harsh winters.

The filling ingredients are tossed with a little cornflour or flour: these thicken the fruit juice during cooking and produce a texture that harmonises better with the topping. Sugar is a matter of taste, but peaches and berries are sweet, so be cautious. Maple syrup is a favourite sweetener for rustic blueberry cobblers.

Flavourings such as spices are not routinely added to cobbler fillings, but try lemon or orange zest, or a hint of clove, cinnamon or vanilla if you like them. Or try a flavoured spirit or liqueur: bourbon added to peaches or sloe gin to plums or damsons.

A generous filling is good in a cobbler, so use a deep dish. Scone or soft biscuit dough should be rolled or pressed out to about 2–2.5cm thick. Softer doughs are dropped over the fruit or savoury base from a spoon; they find their own level during baking. In common with crumbles, cobblers – especially fruit-based ones – are prone to boiling over and an oven tray underneath is essential.

Cobbler toppings must be fully cooked. If in doubt, check the underneath of a biscuit or dumpling at the end of the baking time. If the base seems to be batter-like and not fully distinct from the filling, return it to the oven for 5–10 minutes.

Pear Cobbler

Pears combine beautifully with lemon and almonds in this recipe.

About 1kg cooking pears
60g caster sugar, preferably
   vanilla sugar
Juice of 1 lemon (preferably unwaxed)
   and the zest cut into thin strips
2 teaspoons cornflour
FOR THE TOPPING
150g plain flour

2 teaspoons baking powder
50g ground almonds
60g butter
60g honey
1–2 drops almond essence
About 100ml milk
1–2 tablespoons demerara sugar

Preheat the oven to 190°C.

Peel and core the pears, then cut into small chunks and put into a pan with the sugar, lemon juice and zest and about 150ml water. Cook gently until the pears are soft enough to be roughly mashed with a fork. Slake the cornflour with a little water, stir into the mix and bring to the boil until it clears and thickens. Pour into a baking dish which leaves at least a couple of centimetres depth to spare.

To make the topping, mix the flour, baking powder and ground almonds. Put the butter and honey in a small saucepan over a low heat. Stir until the butter has just melted and the honey is liquid. Add a drop or two of almond essence. Stir this into the flour mixture, immediately followed by the milk, and stir just enough to form a thick batter. Drop this in generous spoonfuls over the pear mixture.

Put the dish on an oven tray and bake for 20–25 minutes or until the top is golden and the topping is fully cooked. If it is browning too fast, turn the heat down and cook for a little longer. Serve warm with vanilla ice cream or crème fraîche.

Creeping Crust Cobbler

A recipe for those with a sweet tooth, this is a cross between a cobbler and a pie and is very easy to make. The topping mixture creeps over the fruit as it bakes, hence the name. Plums, peaches, damsons, strawberries and blackberries are all good in this recipe.

100g butter

150g plain flour

2 teaspoons baking powder

200g granulated sugar

120ml milk

About 400g plums, stoned

Preheat the oven to 180°C.

Use a large, relatively deep dish. Put the butter in the dish and put it into the oven to melt, about 5 minutes. Remove.

Mix the flour, baking powder and sugar together, then pour in the milk. Stir just enough to make a thick batter. It is important not to over-work the mixture. Spoon the batter evenly over the melted butter. Distribute the plums over the top. Put the dish on an oven tray, return to the oven and bake for 30–40 minutes. The batter will rise to the surface, forming a crust. Make sure it's fully cooked underneath. Serve warm with vanilla ice cream.

Blackcurrant Buckle

Not quite cobbler, not quite cake, this is a north American recipe, ideal for gluts of summer berries from garden or allotment. Blueberries are the usual fruit, but blackcurrants work well, their tart juiciness contrasting with the cake.

FOR THE TOPPING
60g soft brown sugar
60g plain flour
1 teaspoon ground cinnamon or
    mixed spice
60g butter, cut into cubes

CAKE MIX
60g butter, softened
60g caster sugar, plus extra for
    dredging (optional)
1 egg
140g self-raising flour (or 140g plain
    flour and 1½ teaspoons baking
    powder)
½ teaspoon salt
About 80ml milk
About 250g blackcurrants

Preheat the oven to 180°C.

Butter a baking dish about 22cm square.

To make the topping, mix the brown sugar, plain flour, cinnamon or spice, and rub in the butter. Chill.

For the cake, cream the butter and sugar together until pale and fluffy. Beat in the egg. Mix in half of the flour and the salt, then half of the milk, then the remaining flour and milk. The batter should be quite soft. Spread it in a baking dish and scatter the blackcurrants over it; they should go right to the edge of the dish. Crumble the topping mixture between your fingers and distribute this over the fruit, again right to the edge. Bake for 35–40 minutes.

Leave to cool a little. Sprinkle with extra sugar if desired. Serve with ice cream, cream or custard.

Blueberry Slump

A traditional pudding from Nova Scotia and New England, originally cooked on the stove top, steaming the dough. Lemon zest is a good addition to the topping.

400–500g blueberries, bilberries, blackberries or a mixture of summer berries
100g granulated sugar
Juice of ½ a lemon

FOR THE TOPPING
250g plain flour
1 teaspoon baking powder
20g granulated sugar
Finely grated zest of 1 lemon (optional)
120g butter, cut into cubes
1 egg
About 150ml milk

Preheat the oven to 220°C.

Put the berries, sugar and lemon juice in a baking dish (about 5–7cm deep) and stir. Cover with foil, place on an oven tray and bake for 10–15 minutes, until the fruit is soft.

To make the topping, mix the flour, baking powder, sugar and lemon zest, if using. Rub in the butter until the mixture resembles fine breadcrumbs. Break the egg into a measuring jug and make up to 200ml with milk. Whisk together. Stir into the flour mixture to make a sticky dough.

Use two spoons to drop 12 rough ovals of dough on top of the berries. Cover and return, on the tray, to the oven for 15 minutes. Uncover and bake for another 10–15 minutes or until the topping is fully cooked underneath. Remove from the oven and leave to rest for 10 minutes. Serve with ice cream, thick cream or custard.

Grunts, Slumps, Buckles and Sonkers

Grunts, slumps, buckles and sonkers are variations on cobblers, made down the east coast of North America. Starting in the north, grunts or slumps are associated with Nova Scotia and New England. They consist of cooked fruit – blueberries are a favourite – topped with spoonfuls of dough, often called dumplings. These supposedly make little grunting noises as they steam on top or slump in an amorphous mass when the pudding is served, giving the names to the puddings. Fans of Louisa May Alcott's *Little Women* may remember that the family house was called Apple Slump, perhaps a wry reference to a failed orchard business, or perhaps an affectionate nod to the local pudding.

Buckles seem to be called such because the surface sags and undulates. The name is used for something that is a cross between a cake and a pudding, a plain cake mixture beneath a generous scattering of fruit (blueberries are the usual choice); a crumble topping may be added. Perhaps they emerged as a way to make plain cakes more interesting or maybe they are related to the fruit and sponge puddings of British tradition, such as Eve's pudding , which consists of apples under a sponge layer.

Sonkers, the most mysterious of this band, are unique to North Carolina. Beyond the fact that they are baked fruit-based puddings involving some kind of pastry, cooks do not agree about recipes. They can be double-crust, or top crust only, latticed or plain, or have a layer of pastry in the middle. They may be filled with berries, stone fruit, rhubarb or (a North Carolina favourite) sweet potato. Are they called sonkers because the top tends to sink under the juice? Or are they really fruit pies, transformed by local traditions?

Apple Pandowdy

A delicious autumn or winter pudding from New England.

About 1.5kg apples – a firm eating
  variety such as Granny Smith's
60g butter
30g muscovado sugar
1 generous tablespoon golden syrup
Finely grated zest and juice of
  ½ a lemon
1 teaspoon vanilla essence or paste

1 generous teaspoon mixed spice
¼ teaspoon salt
2 tablespoons apple cider vinegar
Flour for dusting
250g puff pastry (bought or
  home-made)
Milk, cream or beaten egg to glaze
2 tablespoons demerara sugar

Preheat the oven to 220°C.

Peel and core the apples and cut into slices about 5mm thick. Put the butter in a skillet (or an ordinary frying pan) and melt, then heat it until the foam has subsided and it gives off a nutty smell. Mix in the syrup, lemon juice and zest, vanilla, spice, salt and cider vinegar. Pour over the apples and toss them in the mixture. Return to the skillet, if it is ovenproof, or tip into a baking dish.

Dust a work surface with flour and roll out the pastry. Use it to cover the apples, tucking it in around the edges. Brush with milk, cream or egg and scatter the demerara sugar over the top. Place on an oven tray and bake for 20 minutes.

Remove from the oven and cut through the pastry to make squares roughly 4 x 4cm. Press the edges of the pastry squares down into the juices. Leave to rest for about 10 minutes. Turn the heat down to 180°C and return to the oven. Cook for another 20–30 minutes, by which time the apples should be soft and the filling bubbling.

Remove from the oven (remember that a skillet handle will be very hot). Serve with thick cream or ice cream.

Pandowdy

Pandowdy is firmly associated with New England. Made from apples, spiced and sweetened, traditionally with maple syrup, it is cooked in a skillet (a cast-iron frying pan with an integral cast-iron handle), topped with biscuit dough or pastry, and finished in the oven. Halfway through cooking the crust is cut into pieces and the edges gently pushed into the juice, helping to thicken it. The process is known as dowdying, perhaps because the damaged crust partially soaked in juice looks dowdy. Curiously, the English writer May Byron, in her book *Pot-Luck* (1914), recorded a version of apple dowdy from Essex: a baking dish lined with thin slices of bread and butter, filled with apples, syrup and some water, spiced with nutmeg, covered with more bread and butter, and baked for about 2 hours.

Berry Cobbler with Sour Cream Biscuits

Sour cream gives a subtle but distinctive buttery richness to this cobbler topping, based on southern-USA-style soft biscuits. It can be made with strawberries alone, if preferred.

600g berries – use about 300g
    strawberries and add raspberries,
    blueberries or bilberries,
    blackcurrants and redcurrants
    according to availability and taste
50g granulated sugar
A little grated lemon or lime zest
    and juice
1 tablespoon cornflour

FOR THE BISCUIT TOPPING
175g plain flour, plus extra for dusting
50g granulated sugar
1½ teaspoons baking powder
60g butter, chilled
100ml sour cream
A little milk
Demerara sugar

Preheat the oven to 190°C.

Pick over and wash the berries. Hull the strawberries and cut into halves or quarters if they are large. Put all the berries, the sugar, zest and juice and the cornflour into a bowl and toss together, then pour into the dish in which you intend to bake the cobbler. Cover with foil and bake for about 15 minutes.

While the berries warm through, make the biscuit topping. Mix the flour, sugar and baking powder. Coarsely grate the butter directly into the mixture (dip it in the flour from time to time if it tends to clog the grater). Stir to distribute it evenly. Stir in the sour cream, mixing well with a fork. If the dough seems on the dry side, add milk a teaspoon at a time until everything comes together. Turn out onto a floured surface and knead gently for six to eight turns to even out the dough. Then roll or pat out to about 2cm thick and cut out eight 5cm rounds, gathering and re-rolling the trimmings if necessary.

Remove the berries from the oven, discard the foil and arrange the biscuits on top. Brush them with a little milk and scatter a little demerara sugar over the top. Put the dish on an oven tray and bake for 25 minutes or until the topping is fully cooked. Serve warm with ice cream or sour cream.

Crumble Tarts and Cakes

Apple Cake with Crumble Topping

This is based on the National Trust's Killerton cider and apple cake, given the crumble top treatment. The original cake uses cider made on the 200-year-old press at the Killerton estate in Devon, and flour from Clyston Mill on the estate – if these aren't to hand use your preferred cider and plain white flour.

---

1 large cooking apple, peeled, cored and chopped

50g sultanas

150ml cider (or cold tea)

110g butter, softened

110g soft brown sugar

2 eggs

225g plain flour

1 heaped teaspoon baking powder

1 teaspoon ground cinnamon

Grated zest of 1 lemon

FOR THE TOPPING

70g plain flour

40g porridge oats

30g walnuts, finely chopped

100g golden caster or soft pale brown sugar

1 teaspoon mixed spice

80g butter, melted and cooled but still liquid

Put the apple, sultanas and cider into a bowl. Mix well and leave to macerate for about 30 minutes.

To make the topping, mix the flour, oats, walnuts, sugar and spice. Drizzle in the butter, stirring with a fork to make a crumbly mixture. Chill.

Preheat the oven to 180°C.

Grease or line a deep 20 cm diameter cake tin.

Cream the butter and sugar together until pale and fluffy. Beat in the eggs one at a time. Mix the flour, baking powder and cinnamon and stir in. Add the lemon zest, the macerated apples, sultanas and cider and mix well. Scrape the mixture into the cake tin, levelling the top.

Break up the topping mixture into small pieces and distribute in an even layer over the cake mixture. Bake for 45–60 minutes. Leave to cool in the tin before turning out and serving.

Apples

From the humblest cottage to the grandest stately home, nearly all households in England, Wales and Northern Ireland once grew an apple tree, or two, or dozens. They provided fruit for the table, for cooking, and for cider (for the latter, visit National Trust sites in the south-west, especially Barrington Court in Somerset). Hundreds of varieties developed, some known only in very restricted localities, others hugely successful and grown in large commercial orchards. Although the oldest varieties have a history that goes back to the seventeenth century or earlier, interest in plants and gardens in the eighteenth and nineteenth centuries vastly expanded the range of apples available.

Gardeners and growers vied with each other to raise novel varieties for dessert or kitchen, or give interesting nuances of texture or flavour. One example among many was the Egremont Russet, a dessert apple with a rich, nutty flavour and matte brown patches of 'russet' on its skin, thought to have been raised at Petworth (West Sussex) in the late nineteenth century and named for the Egremont family, the owners of the estate.

Different varieties have different seasons for ripening. Although they are considered autumn fruit, some apples are available by July. Others are 'keepers', picked late and ripened slowly in cool, frost-proof stores. By clever planting, Victorian gardeners ensured that apples were available in every month except May and June. Many houses had a space for keeping them in winter; the Old Apple Store at Brockhampton in Herefordshire is now the tea room.

Lots of National Trust houses have apple orchards, which are lovely places to visit. In spring enjoy the burst of pink-white blossom, and later in the year the bounty of ripening fruit. Autumn is an ideal time to find out more, as many host Apple Day events. Non-commercial varieties of the fruit are displayed and can often be tasted, a revelation after the limited number of commercial ones stocked by supermarkets. They are often for sale, allowing the cook to experiment; so it's well worth going along, tasting the fruit on offer and talking to the experts – and maybe coming away with a bag of fruit.

National Trust locations notable for apples (among many) include Clumber Park (Nottinghamshire), home to an orchard with over 72 varieties; Croome (Worcestershire), which has old cider apple trees and newer plantings of historic varieties from the 1700s and 1800s; the diamond-trained espaliered apple trees at Coughton Court (Warwickshire), beautiful displays of the gardener's skill; Gunby (Lincolnshire), where 54 varieties are grown and one can walk a pergola line of apple trees; Cotehele (Cornwall), whose historic orchard boasts many rare varieties; Errdig (North Wales), home to a long-running autumn apple festival; Acorn Bank (Cumbria), which has a recently established orchard and a collection of over 100 local varieties; Nunnington Hall (North Yorkshire), with apple trees planted on either side of the front lawn; and Ardress House in County Armargh, where Apple Sundays – days celebrating, cooking and eating the fruit – are held in the autumn.

Apples and apple-related customs run deep in the British Isles. Avalon, of the King Arthur myth, means the Isle of Apples, and many games relating to apples are traditional to Halloween. Costermonger, an old word for a street seller of fruit, originally meant an apple seller (from the word 'costard', the name of an apple well known in the Middle Ages). And to be the apple of someone's eye is, of course, to be adored. One very special apple tree, an example of an ancient variety known as the Flower of Kent (whose fruit served as both a cooking and an eating apple), can be seen at Woolsthorpe Manor in Lincolnshire: perhaps if Isaac Newton had not been sitting under the tree pondering why objects always fall to the ground, the theory of gravity would have taken somewhat longer to emerge.

Dutch Apple Tart

Recipes of this type are sometimes called Dutch, Polish or Irish apple tart or apple cake. Who do they really belong to? What matters is that they are good.

300g (made weight) shortcrust pastry
    (bought or home-made)
FOR THE TOPPING
130g plain flour, plus extra for dusting
90g soft pale brown sugar
120g butter, cut into cubes

FOR THE FILLING
About 1kg apples – an eating variety
    such as Cox's Orange Pippin
Juice of 1 lemon
100g granulated sugar
20g plain flour
¼ teaspoon ground cinnamon
1 tablespoon demerara sugar

Preheat the oven to 200°C.

On a floured work surface, roll out the pastry and ease it into a pie dish about 23cm in diameter. Trim and flute the edges. Chill while you prepare the topping and filling.

To make the topping, mix the flour and brown sugar. Rub in the butter until the mixture resembles fine breadcrumbs.

To make the filling, peel, quarter and core the apples. Cut them into thin slices and toss in lemon juice. Mix the granulated sugar, flour and cinnamon and stir into the apples. Pile this mixture into the pastry case, heaping it up in the centre. Distribute the topping evenly over the apple mixture, and finish by sprinkling over the demerara sugar.

Bake for 45–60 minutes or until cracks appear in the surface of the crumble and juice starts to bubble through, indicating that the apples are soft. If the top is browning too fast, turn the heat down and cook for a little longer.

Leave to cool for at least 2 hours before eating. Sour cream is good with this.

Toffee and Pear Crumble Tart

'Total self indulgence' is how Sarah Edington describes the apple version of this tart in *National Trust Classic British Cooking*.

FOR THE PASTRY

225g plain flour, plus extra for dusting

4 tablespoons caster sugar

110g butter, cut into cubes, plus extra for greasing

4 egg yolks

FOR THE FILLING

50g butter

75g soft brown sugar

150ml golden syrup

150ml double cream

2 drops vanilla essence

900g cooking pears, such as Conference

FOR THE CRUMBLE

110g plain flour

110g porridge oats

75g butter, cut into cubes

75g soft brown sugar

Preheat the oven to 180°C.

Butter a 25 cm diameter flan tin.

First, make the pastry: sift the flour and sugar together, rub in the butter and stir in the egg yolks to bind the dough. Roll out on a floured work surface and line the flan tin. Prick the bottom and then chill.

To make the filling, melt the butter in a saucepan over a very low heat, add the sugar and golden syrup and heat very gently, stirring well to dissolve the sugar, for 5 minutes. Stir in the cream and the vanilla, beat well until the sauce is smooth, then leave to cool until lukewarm.

Peel, core and slice the pears thinly. Arrange over the pastry. Pour the filling over the pears.

To make the crumble, mix the flour and oats and rub in the butter until the mixture is crumbly. Stir in the sugar and then spread the mixture evenly over the filling. Bake for 30–40 minutes, until the top is golden brown and crunchy.

Pears

Pears, like apples, are an important orchard tree in Britain. They come in many different varieties for eating and cooking, and provide juice for a fermented alcoholic drink known as perry.

Their geographical spread as a common fruit tree is more limited than that of apples as they flower early in the spring. For the gardener this leads to much anxiety about frost and poor cropping. They grow best in areas where spring tends to come a little earlier, such as the Severn Valley and Somerset, but this did not stop households in other areas growing them, often trained on walls or wires in sheltered kitchen gardens. The walled garden at Beningbrough Hall (North Yorkshire) has particularly nice examples of this, the pears trained on arches over the main path; the Round Garden at Cliveden (Buckinghamshire) follows a similar principle. Another National Trust garden that includes pear trees is Dyrham Park (Gloucestershire, traditional pear-growing country): visit in the autumn for pear-related events.

As a fruit for cooked desserts, pears lack the sweet–acid balance that makes apples such a success, but make up for it with their texture and sweet perfumed flesh. They combine well with apples, quinces, almonds or hazelnuts, and ginger, especially stem ginger. Pear trees grow tall and can be conspicuous in the landscape. In the past, these fruit were much more important for cooking and preserving than they are now. There are many traditional varieties with a long history and localised specimens. A hard variety used for cooking and known as Warden pears (named for Wardon Abbey in Bedfordshire, where they were grown) was important in the fifteenth and sixteenth centuries: 'I must have saffron, to colour the warden pies', says the clown in Shakespeare's play *A Winter's Tale*. The old pear variety known as Black Worcester may be an example of the Warden type; see them growing in the orchard at Croome, near Worcester.

Rhubarb and Orange Crumble Tart

Pink forced rhubarb is lovely in this, but outdoor rhubarb can be used later in the year.

300g plain flour, plus extra for dusting
100g icing sugar
Grated zest of 1 orange (keep the
  orange for the filling)
Seeds scraped from ½ a vanilla pod
150g butter, cut into cubes

1 egg, beaten
600g rhubarb (trimmed weight),
  washed
1 tablespoon cornflour
60–80g caster sugar

Preheat the oven to 180°C.

You will need a 25 cm diameter flan tin with a removable base.

Mix the flour, icing sugar, orange zest and vanilla. Rub in the butter until the mixture resembles fine breadcrumbs. Add most of the egg to the mixture, stirring and pulling the pieces together to make a dough. Try not to make it sticky, but add all the egg if it seems to be dry. Once it has come together, chill in the fridge for about 30 minutes.

Take a generous third of the dough and roll out on a floured work surface to make a circle big enough to line the flan tin. Ease the dough into the tin, prick the bottom with a fork and trim the edges. Line with a square of greaseproof paper and fill with baking beans. Bake for 15 minutes, then remove the paper and beans and return to the oven for a further 10 minutes (keep an eye on it and turn down the heat if it shows signs of browning at the edges).

If the rhubarb stems are thick, cut in half lengthways, then cut across in 1cm lengths. Cut the remaining peel, including the white pith, off the orange and use a small knife to slip the flesh out of the segments, then add them to the rhubarb. Add the cornflour and sugar to taste, and stir together. Pile the fruit mixture into the baked tart case and then crumble the remaining pastry mix over the top.

Bake for 30–40 minutes or until the rhubarb is soft. If the pastry at the edges is browning too quickly, protect it with strips of foil.

Remove from the oven and leave to cool for 15–20 minutes before serving with crème fraîche, whipped cream or crème anglaise.

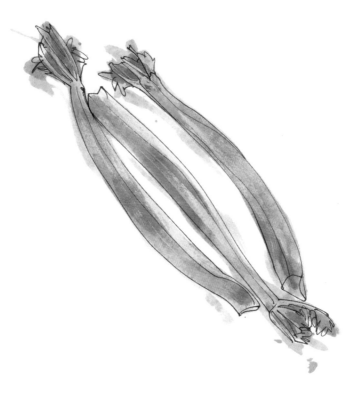

Zwetschgenkuchen, or Plum Crumble Cake

This unusual German cake has a yeast dough base and a streusel crumble topping. If using dried yeast, follow the manufacturer's instructions. Warmth is essential for the dough to rise well.

15g fresh yeast (available from supermarket bakeries)
250g strong plain white flour, plus extra for handling
75g granulated sugar
Pinch of salt
30g butter, melted, plus extra for greasing
1 egg, beaten
A few drops vanilla essence

FOR THE PLUM LAYER
About 750g plums
½ teaspoon ground cinnamon
sugar (optional)

FOR THE STREUSEL TOPPING
60g plain flour
80g soft pale brown sugar
60g butter, melted

Warm 60ml of milk until hand hot and add the yeast. Set aside for a few minutes until frothy.

Mix the flour, sugar and salt, preferably in the bowl of a food mixer or processor. (This is a heavy mixture to handle without a machine – it is too soft to knead, and has to be beaten with the hand.) Add the yeast mixture, the melted butter, the egg and the vanilla. Mix or process to make a thick mixture in between a dough and a batter, adding a little more milk if it seems dry. Don't over-process. Cover the mixture and leave in a warm place to rise for about an hour.

Stone the plums and cut in eighths lengthways. Lavishly butter a shallow baking tin, at least 18 x 30cm, preferably a little larger.

When the dough mixture has doubled in size, flour your fingers and ease it into the buttered tin. Pat out the dough, dipping your fingers in flour every so often, to make an even layer that fills the base of the tin. Pack the pieces of plum in close-set lines across the top. Dust with the cinnamon. If the fruit seems sour or under-ripe, add a little sugar, but be cautious as this can produce too much juice. Leave in a warm place to prove for about an hour.

Preheat the oven to 180°C.

To make the streusel topping, mix the flour and sugar and gradually add the butter, stirring all the time, to make a crumbly mixture.

After proving, scatter the streusel over the plums in an even layer. Bake for 30–35 minutes until the dough is golden brown and the plums are cooked and exuding juice.

Leave to cool in the tin for at least 10 minutes, longer if possible, before cutting into 12 pieces. Serve alone or with crème fraîche.

Streusel

Streusel is a central European type of crumble. The name derives from the German verb *streuen*, to strew. It contains a lower proportion of flour than British crumble mixture and is usually flavoured with cinnamon. In Germany and central Europe it is used for cakes, scattered in layers in the middle and over the top.

Streusel has become extremely popular in the USA. As a topping on coffee cakes (semi-sweet cakes eaten with coffee, often for breakfast – not cakes flavoured with coffee) and on muffins and cheesecakes it is something of an obsession, with home bakers vying to make the best. It is also marbled through cake batter, crumbled over creamy desserts and used to top apple pies.

Gooseberry Custard Crumble Cake

This is loosely based on an apple streusel cake from *Festive Baking in Austria, Germany and Switzerland* by Sarah Kelly, a wonderful book for anyone interested in baking.

FOR THE FILLING
500g gooseberries
30g caster sugar
1 teaspoon cornflour
2 teaspoons Sambuca, Pernod or other anise-flavoured spirit or liqueur (optional)

FOR THE CAKE
230g plain flour
100g caster sugar

20g custard powder
Seeds scraped from ½ a vanilla pod
1 large egg
1½ teaspoons baking powder
130g butter, melted and cooled but still liquid
200ml ready-made custard (home-made or bought from the chilled cabinet)
Icing sugar and whipped cream to serve (optional)

Preheat the oven to 180°C.

Grease and line the base and sides of a deep 20cm cake tin with a removable base.

To make the filling (this can be done in advance), put the gooseberries into a pan with a tablespoon of water and cook gently until soft: they will inevitably break up. Simmer gently to evaporate some of the liquid. Add the sugar; mix the cornflour with a teaspoon of water and stir in. Add the Sambuca, if using, and leave to cool.

For the cake, mix the flour, sugar, custard powder and vanilla. Beat the egg with the baking powder and pour into the centre of the mixture. Pour in the butter in a thin stream, stirring constantly to make a crumbly dough. Take a generous half of this and press it over

the bottom of the lined cake tin. Bring it up the sides a little. Spoon
the gooseberry mixture over the top, then spoon the custard over this.
It's better not to take it too close to the edge. Crumble the remaining
cake mixture over the top.

Place the cake tin on an oven tray and bake for 40–45 minutes.
Remove from the oven and leave to cool for at least 30 minutes, longer
if possible. Remove from the tin and peel off the baking paper. Sift
icing sugar over and serve with whipped cream.

Gooseberries

Gooseberries grow easily in Britain. Visitors to Hanbury Hall, near Droitwich (Worcestershire) in early summer may be fortunate enough to buy some of the ones grown in the walled garden there. They come early in the year, around the end of May, a welcome sight in the past when little other seasonal fruit was available. They are a fruit with a quirky history, something of a British, or more specifically English, speciality. In the eighteenth century they were grown in the gardens of large houses for making preserves, but they also became a standby of cottage gardens and a fruit that was grown competitively by working men.

In the middle of this century, weavers in Lancashire founded gooseberry clubs. These soon spread to Cheshire, the Midlands and Yorkshire and in the nineteenth century over 150 gooseberry shows were held at different locations. The aim of the competition was to produce the heaviest berry, weighed down to half a grain in the troy weight system (which is principally used for precious stones and weighs down to minute fractions of a gram). Annual gooseberry shows are still held in Cheshire, and one also survives at Egton Bridge in Yorkshire. Fortunately for the cook, there were also plenty of ordinary berries for preserving and for puddings.

Gooseberries are one of the best fruits for crumbles, breaking down to a rough purée with a tart acidity that combines deliciously with sweet crumble toppings. Vanilla, elderflower and aniseed liqueurs go well with them, as do creamy or custardy accompaniments.

Sbrisolona, or Italian Crumble Cake

A favourite in Lombardy, this is a cross between shortbread and crumble. Adding fruit is not traditional, but the combination of quince and rose water is delicious with the cake.

---

1 quince, weighing about 350g

75g caster sugar

1 teaspoon rose water

Grappa or vin santo, to serve
   (optional)

FOR THE CAKE

100g almonds, skin on

100g plain flour

100g cornmeal/polenta (quick-cook
   polenta is fine)

50g granulated sugar

50g soft brown sugar

Pinch of salt

100g butter, cut into cubes

1 egg yolk

A few drops almond essence

6–8 almonds, skin on, to decorate

Preheat the oven to 160°C.

Line a shallow cake tin about 23cm in diameter with baking paper.

Cut the quince into eight and remove the core (no need to peel). Put the pieces in a small baking dish and add the caster sugar and 100ml water. Cover and bake for 1 hour, then uncover and bake for a further hour or until the quince is soft and a pink-gold colour. Add more water if it seems to be drying out, but by the end of cooking only about 2 tablespoons should be left. Remove from the oven, leave to cool a little and remove the skin. Mash the flesh with the cooking juices and the rose water.

While the quince cooks, prepare the cake: this is best done in a food processor. Roughly chop the almonds. Mix the flour, cornmeal, sugars and salt and add to the almonds. Process briefly to mix. Add the butter and pulse until the mixture resembles breadcrumbs, then add the egg yolk and almond essence and blend briefly. (If you don't have a food processor, mix the flour, cornmeal, sugars and salt, and rub in the butter. Chop the almonds roughly and stir in, then add the egg yolk and essence).

Pack about half the mixture over the base of the prepared tin. Spread the quince mixture over, leaving a clear border of about 2cm around the edge. Cover with the rest of the mixture, squeezing a little to make irregular lumps on top.

Scatter 6–8 whole almonds over the top.

Bake for 40–50 minutes, until golden. Remove from the oven and leave to cool completely. Break into pieces, rather than cutting it.

The Italians like to sprinkle this cake with grappa or drink a glass of vin santo with it, but it's also good with tea or coffee.

Crumble Variations: Sbrisolona

Most countries have some kind of pastry or cake in their repertoire which is short, crisp and crumbly (think Scottish shortbread). *Sbrisolona*, also known as *sbriciolata*, is the north Italian version. It is crisp and extremely crumbly – and very moreish. Originally associated with Mantova (Mantua) in Lombardy, it is now found in the *pasticceria* (pastry shops) in many towns in the surrounding area. The recipe is unusual because it includes cornmeal among the ingredients. Locals claim that it originated as something baked by poor people and that almonds and generous amounts of butter were added to the recipe by wealthier families.

The name comes from a dialect word that means crumb or crumbly. The texture is reminiscent of shortbread, but the cornmeal gives it an interesting, slightly gritty texture and a distinctive flavour. Fruit fillings are not traditional, although there are some recipes in Italian for *sbrisolona* with apple filling. Try softening some chocolate hazelnut spread over hot water and using a generous layer of this in place of the quince.

Chocolate Chip Crumb Cake

Crumb cakes, also known as coffee cakes (made to accompany coffee) are very popular in the USA. Eat with morning coffee, or as an afternoon teatime treat.

FOR THE CRUMB TOPPING
160g plain flour
75g soft pale brown sugar
75g granulated sugar
1 scant teaspoon ground cinnamon
100g butter, melted and cooled but
    still liquid

FOR THE CAKE
75g butter, softened
100g caster sugar
1 egg
150g plain flour (it is worth seeking
    out extra-fine sponge flour for this)
1 ½ teaspoons baking powder
Pinch of salt
150ml buttermilk or natural yoghurt
50g dark chocolate chips
25g candied orange peel, cut into very
    fine dice

Preheat the oven to 180°C.

Line a 20 cm square cake tin with baking paper.

To make the crumb topping, mix together the flour, both sugars, and the cinnamon. Drizzle in the melted butter, stirring with a fork to make a crumbly mixture. Set aside.

To make the cake, cream the butter and sugar together until pale and fluffy. Add the egg and beat for another 2–3 minutes. Sift the flour, baking powder and salt together and add in thirds to the creamed mixture, alternating with the buttermilk or yoghurt and stirring well between each addition: the result should be a soft but stiff-ish batter (add a little milk if it seems over-stiff). Fold in the chocolate chips and orange peel.

Spoon the batter into the cake tin, levelling it with a knife. Spread the crumb mixture over the top as evenly as possible. Bake for 35–45 minutes or until a cocktail stick inserted in the centre comes out clean. If it is browning too quickly, protect the surface with a piece of baking paper. If there is any doubt about how well the cake is done, turn down the heat a little and cook for 5–10 minutes longer.

Leave to cool in the tin for at least 30 minutes before removing and cutting.

Crumble Muffins and Slices

Lemon Curd Crumble Muffins

Lemon and almonds have always been popular ingredients in traditional British cooking. If you don't make lemon curd at home, the National Trust sells their own version.

FOR THE ALMOND CRUMBLE TOPPING
100g plain flour
40g ground almonds, or almond flour
80g granulated sugar
Finely grated zest of ½ an unwaxed
  lemon
80g butter, melted and cooled but
  still liquid
1 drop almond essence

FOR THE MUFFINS
180g plain flour
2 teaspoons baking powder
100g granulated sugar
2 eggs
100g natural yoghurt
Finely grated zest of ½ an unwaxed
  lemon
1 drop almond essence
180g butter, melted and cooled but
  still liquid
120g lemon curd

Preheat the oven to 180°C.

Line two muffin tins with standard cupcake cases.

To make the crumble topping, mix the flour, almonds and sugar. Add the lemon zest to the butter along with a drop of almond essence, then pour into the dry ingredients, stirring until it has the consistency of fine breadcrumbs. Set aside.

To make the muffins, mix the flour, baking powder and sugar in a mixing bowl. In a separate bowl or jug, mix the eggs, yoghurt, lemon zest and almond essence together, then stir in the butter. Don't worry if the mixture looks a little curdled. Stir into the dry ingredients until fully incorporated, but don't overmix. Stir the lemon curd to soften.

If it seems a little on the stiff side, add a teaspoon or two of warm water. Quickly stir it through the muffin batter.

Divide the mixture between the muffin cases: they should be about half full, no more. Spoon over the almond crumble. Bake for about 20 minutes or until a cocktail stick inserted in the centre comes out clean. Best eaten while still warm.

Spiced Pumpkin Muffins
with Crumble Topping

In Britain, pumpkins were grown mostly for their handsome looks – visit Slindon (West Sussex) in autumn to see a wonderful range. The unusual spicing is from an early pumpkin recipe in *The Compleat Cook* (1655). Use mixed spice if preferred.

350g slice of pumpkin, deseeded
80g wholemeal flour
80g plain flour
100g soft pale brown sugar
1 teaspoon bicarbonate of soda
1 teaspoon baking powder
Pinch of salt
½ teaspoon ground cinnamon
½ teaspoon grated nutmeg
½ teaspoon ground cloves
½ teaspoon coarsely ground
    black pepper
180g butter, melted and cooled
    but still liquid
2 eggs
1 medium eating apple, peeled
    and grated

FOR THE CRUMBLE TOPPING
80g plain flour
60g granulated sugar
30g butter, melted and cooled but
    still liquid
50g walnuts, chopped

Preheat the oven to 210°C.

Wrap the pumpkin in foil and bake for 1 hour or until soft. Discard the skin and mash the flesh; you should have about 225g of pumpkin purée. Set aside.

Turn the oven down to 180°C. Line two muffin tins with standard cupcake cases.

To make the crumble topping: mix the flour and sugar in a bowl, then pour in the melted butter in a thin stream, stirring constantly to make a breadcrumb-like texture. Stir in the walnuts. Set aside.

To make the muffins mix the flours, brown sugar, bicarbonate of soda, baking powder, salt and spices together in a mixing bowl. In a separate bowl, mix the pumpkin purée, melted butter, eggs and grated apple. Combine the two mixtures and stir well. Divide this mixture between the muffin cases. Then spoon some of the crumble topping over each one, pressing it down slightly. Bake for 15 minutes or until a cocktail stick inserted in the centre comes out clean. Leave to cool a little before eating.

Blueberry Muffins with Cinnamon Streusel

Use either cultivated blueberries or foraged wild bilberries for this North American-inspired recipe.

FOR THE STREUSEL TOPPING
120g plain flour
80g granulated sugar
1 teaspoon ground cinnamon
80g butter, melted and cooled but
     still liquid

FOR THE MUFFINS
250g plain flour, plus extra for dusting
3 teaspoons baking powder
120g granulated sugar
1 scant teaspoon salt
2 eggs
300ml sour cream
100ml neutral-flavoured oil, such as
     grapeseed, sunflower or rapeseed
1 teaspoon vanilla essence
300g blueberries or bilberries

Preheat the oven to 200°C.

Line two muffin tins with standard cupcake cases.

First, make the streusel topping: mix the flour, sugar and cinnamon, then drizzle in the melted butter, stirring constantly to form a lumpy mixture. Set aside.

To make the muffins, mix the flour, baking powder, sugar and salt in a mixing bowl. In a separate bowl, beat the eggs with the sour cream, oil and vanilla. Combine the two mixtures. Take about 200g of the berries and dust with a little flour. Fold into the muffin mixture. (Bilberries are softer and squashier than blueberries, making the batter purple, so don't over-mix.)

Divide the mixture between the muffin cases. Top each one with a few of the reserved berries, then with the streusel mixture, pressing it down slightly. Bake for 15–20 minutes or until a cocktail stick inserted in the centre comes out clean. Leave to cool a little before eating.

Blueberries and Bilberries

Blueberries (*Vaccinium corymbosum*) are of North American origin and are relatives of the bilberry (*Vaccinium myrtillus*), which is native to Europe. Blueberries are the fruit of choice for many North American cobblers and cakes with streusel or crumble toppings. Cultivated varieties of blueberries, grown in various countries, are the ones that line our supermarket shelves – 'blueberries as big as the end of your thumb', as the poet Robert Frost wrote.

In Britain it is worth looking for the blueberry's wild relatives, known as bilberries, whortleberries and various other regional names. They grow on heathlands and acid-soiled moorlands such as that found around Brimham Rocks and Roseberry Topping in North Yorkshire, Marsden Moor in West Yorkshire and the Long Mynd in Shropshire.

Look for bilberries in late July or August. Take a picnic, hat and sunscreen and spend an afternoon on the moors. Gathering bilberries is a slow task, but to pick a pound or so for muffins or a cobbler shouldn't take long. If boredom sets in, and berries are sparse, even a few are nice mixed with other summer fruit for puddings and cakes. They are smaller than blueberries, with a more acidic, complex flavour and will stain fingers, mouths and clothes purple. This problem can be partially resolved by acquiring a berry comb, a box-like device with a series of wire prongs at the front. Rake this through the bushes in an upward motion, and the berries collect in the enclosed end.

Apricot and Oat Crumble Bars

Crumbles are never going to be health foods, but these crunchy little squares pack in oats, seeds and nuts. Decorate with chocolate (dark, milk or white) if you like.

300g dried apricots
90g plain flour
130g porridge oats
60g soft pale brown sugar
90g butter, cut into cubes

FOR THE TOPPING
60g demerara sugar
60g plain flour
60g butter, melted and cooled but
    still liquid
40g walnuts or pecans,
    coarsely chopped
20g (1½ tablespoons) sunflower seeds
20g (1½ tablespoons) pumpkin seeds
10g (1 tablespoon) sesame seeds,
    toasted (see cooking tip on p.78)
50g chocolate, chopped (optional)

The day before, put the apricots into a bowl with just enough water to cover and leave to soak overnight.

Cook the apricots in their soaking water for about 10 minutes (add a little more water if necessary, but don't overdo it). Drain and pulse the apricots in a food processor or coarsely chop to make a rough purée.

Preheat the oven to 180°C.

Line a shallow 20 cm square cake tin with baking paper.

Mix the flour, oats and sugar. Rub in the butter to make a crumbly dough. Press into the base of the tin to make an even layer. Spread the apricot purée over.

For the topping, mix the demerara sugar and flour and stir in the melted butter. Add the nuts and seeds and drop small spoonfuls over the apricots. Bake for 30–40 minutes, until the top is golden. Leave to cool in the tin.

To decorate, melt the chocolate in a bowl over a pan of barely simmering water, then drizzle it in thin lines over the crumble. Chill for about 6 hours or overnight before cutting into 16 pieces.

COOKING TIP To toast sesame seeds, put them in a small heavy frying pan (use no fat) and stir over low heat until they turn golden.

Plums, Peaches and Apricots

Plums are found in numerous varieties. Greengages are the English name for a specific type of plum with sweet, honeyed flesh, named after Sir Thomas Gage, who introduced them to England in the eighteenth century. Damsons are small, richly flavoured plums, with acidic dark red flesh; they have a long but less well-recorded history in Britain. The name is thought to derive from Damascus, where they were believed to originate.

One National Trust location that has revealed a treasure trove in relation to plums is Ickworth, near Bury St Edmunds in Suffolk. A rediscovered gardener's notebook listed over 200 varieties of local plum, gage, pear and apple trees grown there in the early twentieth century, which has provided inspiration for the replanting of Ickworth's walled garden.

Wimpole (Cambridgeshire) also has a fabulous collection of orchard fruit including plums, apples, and pears, and is well worth a visit. The West Midlands was an important plum-growing area and, in recognition of this, the garden at Croome (Worcestershire) has been replanted with local varieties, including Warwickshire Drooper and Pershore (Yellow Egg).

At Brockhampton, visitors can pick their own damsons in late summer. This house is located in Herefordshire, a country historically important for growing damsons. Another area traditionally associated with this fruit is the Lyth Valley in southern Cumbria. Here, near Sizergh, the trees are a feature of local hedgerows, and are a mass of pink blossom in the spring.

Peaches and apricots were the most prized of orchard fruit in big houses, eaten fresh for summer desserts and preserved with sugar for winter. The British climate, even in sheltered areas, can be too unpredictable and chilly for these trees. Wealthy owners of large mansions wanted reliable supplies and built special glasshouses in which to grow them. A good example, in the northernmost part of England, is at Cragside in Northumberland. Here, Lord Armstrong, the former owner of the estate, applied his engineering genius to the Orchard House. This greenhouse, now partially restored, is on a glorious scale: a vast glasshouse for growing pears, citrus fruit, peaches and apricots. The fruit trees grow in pots on cast-iron bases which can be rotated, ensuring symmetrical growth and even ripening, a system that appears to be unique to this site. Under the south-facing terraces that support them runs a system of vents originally intended to transmit hot air, providing warmth for their root-balls, prolonging the fruiting season. Other peach houses include a ruined example at Calke (Derbyshire) and peaches were also grown at Ickworth. At Wimpole a special heated wall was constructed to provide warmth for the peach trees in chilly weather.

All stone fruit are excellent fillings for crumbles and cobblers. Both peaches and apricots make lovely crumble fillings, and peaches – fresh or canned – are the classic North American choice for fruit cobblers. Their flavours harmonise especially well with almonds, flaked, chopped, or used as a flavouring, either as an essence or from crumbled amaretti biscuits.

Apple Cheesecake Crumble Bars

These are sweet and rich, making them perfect for a teatime treat on a blustery autumn day.

About 350g eating apples, peeled
and cored
50g muscovado sugar
30g sultanas
1 teaspoon mixed spice
250g (made weight) shortcrust pastry
(bought or home-made)
250g full fat cream cheese, softened
1 egg
50g caster sugar
A few drops vanilla essence
Finely grated zest of 1 lemon
(preferably unwaxed)

FOR THE TOPPING
50g soft pale brown sugar
50g plain flour
50g porridge oats
50g butter, cut into small cubes

Preheat the oven to 180°C.

Line the base of a shallow cake tin, about 20 x 20cm, with
baking paper.

Cut the apples into roughly 1cm cubes. Put them in a small oven tray
with the muscovado sugar, sultanas and spice and bake for
25 minutes, stirring occasionally.

While the apples are cooking, roll out the pastry and use it to line the
cake tin. Prick the bottom lightly with a fork.

Make the cheesecake filling by whisking together the cream cheese,
egg, caster sugar, vanilla and lemon zest. Set aside.

To make the topping, pulse the pale brown sugar, flour, oats and butter in a food processor to make a crumbly mixture; set aside.

When the apples are cooked, assemble the bars by pouring the cheese mixture into the pastry base. Spoon the fruit over the top, along with any cooking juices. Scatter the crumble topping over the fruit.

Turn the oven down to 160°C and bake for 40–50 minutes, or until the cheese mixture is set. Leave to cool and chill before cutting.

Crumble History

Crumble topping is essentially a sweet mix of flour, sugar and fat, rubbed together to form a mixture that can only be described as crumbly. Mix, sprinkle and bake. There is a great deal to be said for a pudding that can be prepared with speed from easily available ingredients, which everyone loves.

Crumbles have a remarkably short history. They appear to have sprung fully formed into British food habits some time in the first half of the twentieth century. Searches through historic cookbooks are in vain: nothing resembling crumble appears in the chapters devoted to puddings and desserts. The best guess is that they evolved during the Second World War, using whatever fat was available. A leaflet issued by the Ministry of Food in the 1940s apparently introduced the nation to a dish called Scottish Apple Crumble: lightly sweetened apples spiced with cinnamon, cooked under a topping of flour, oats, margarine and sugar. A little short on fat and sugar, as one might expect during rationing, it was probably called a Scottish crumble because the addition of oats suggested an association with Scotland.

The debate has carried on ever since. Do crumble toppings include oats? And if they do, are they crumbles or crisps? One man's crisp can be another man's crumble and it may or may not include oats. However, crisp seems to be a term used more in North America than in Britain. The North American habit of adding crumble toppings to all sorts of cakes probably has roots in German traditions of streusel toppings (page 59).

Crumble is excellent in combination with seasonal fruit that is abundant and easily grown or foraged – apples, pears, plums, blackberries, gooseberries and outdoor rhubarb. The speed and ease with which crumble can be made is of great comfort in an emergency of any kind, let alone wartime. And although butter is an all-time favourite ingredient, it has to be said that the recipe is robust enough to give adequate results using margarine.

The idea was inspired, wherever it came from. It was adopted widely into institutional and domestic catering, a staple of school dinners and family meals. An aura of relief pervaded mid-century school dining halls on days when the pudding was crumble and custard, rather than a pallid suet pudding or glutinous tapioca 'frogspawn'.

Until the 1970s, crumbles always seem to have been sweet and based on the simple original recipe. Innovation got off to a bad start with earnest offerings from wholefood restaurants, made with wholemeal flour and dark brown sugar. These leaden crumbles convinced many who tasted them that such ingredients have no place in crumble-making. Crumbles are not health foods.

Experiments with spices and nuts, adding variety in flavour and texture, came later and the year-round availability of berries and stone fruit has significantly increased variety in fillings.

Deconstructed crumbles, with elements of fruit, crisp topping and creamy accompaniments served separately are a recent innovation. Crumble reached France in 2005 when Camille Le Foll published her book *Crumbles*, a runaway publishing success.

Savoury crumbles were rare until the late twentieth century. One recipe from the early 1980s involved tinned tuna and potato crisps, a useful storecupboard recipe in the days when shops had limited opening hours. They mostly involve cheese. And this raises another question: when does a crumble become a gratin? These classic dishes of French cookery have a long and honourable history. But a gratin topping is a thin layer of breadcrumbs or cheese: it never includes flour. It is the combination of flour and butter that gives character to crumble and, significantly, the French, taking this most British of desserts to heart, know it as *le crumble*.

Christmas Mincemeat and Cranberry Crumble Bars

An alternative to mince pies, using a shortbread-type mixture for the base.

About 120g fresh cranberries

Grated zest and juice of ½ an orange
(preferably unwaxed)

250–300g mincemeat

125g butter, softened

75g caster sugar

250g plain flour

Pinch of salt

Preheat the oven to 180°C.

Line a shallow baking tin, about 18 x 30cm, with baking paper.

Put the cranberries, orange juice and zest in a saucepan and simmer gently for a few minutes, until the berries are soft, then set aside to cool. Stir into the mincemeat.

Cream the butter and sugar together. Sift in the flour and salt and mix well. Take about two thirds of this mixture and spread over the base of the tin, pressing down firmly in an even layer. Spoon the mincemeat mixture over the top and spread out gently, trying not to disturb the base layer. Scatter the remaining butter and flour mixture over the top.

Bake for 15–20 minutes or until the top is pale gold. Leave to cool in the tin, then cut into 12 pieces and store in an airtight tin.

Almond and Berry Crumble Slices

A mixture of summer berries works well for these rich slices. Cut them small as an afternoon teatime treat.

225g self-raising flour
75g ground almonds
Pinch of salt
100g caster sugar
200g butter, cut into cubes
2 egg yolks
A few drops almond essence

400g berries
Juice of ½ a lemon
50g granulated sugar
1 tablespoon cornflour
20g flaked almonds
20g pistachios, coarsely chopped

Mix the flour, ground almonds, salt and caster sugar together, preferably in a food processor. Add the butter and pulse to a crumbly texture. Mix the egg yolks and almond essence and add to the processor, mixing just enough to combine. Empty the mixture into a bowl and press together lightly to form a dough. Chill for 30 minutes.

Preheat the oven to 190°C.

Line a shallow 20 cm square tin with baking paper.

Mix the berries, lemon juice, granulated sugar and cornflour.

Take about three quarters of the dough and press it into the lined tin in an even layer. Spread the berry mixture over the top. Break up the remaining dough into rough pieces and scatter this over the berries. Finish with the flaked almonds and chopped pistachios.

Bake for 50–60 minutes. Check after about 25 minutes and if the top seems to be browning too fast, turn the heat down a little and bake for a few minutes longer.

Leave to cool completely before cutting into 16 squares.

Soft Fruit

All big houses once had their own kitchen gardens. Really good examples now in the care of the National Trust include those at Wimpole (Cambridgeshire), Clumber Park (Nottinghamshire), Attingham Park (Shropshire), Beningbrough (North Yorkshire), Llanerchaeron (Ceredigion) and Tatton Park (Cheshire).

Such gardens grew rows and rows of berries and patches of currant bushes. Exactly what was fashionable depended on the century. Raspberries appear to have been known from medieval times. Redcurrants, blackcurrants and gooseberries were novelties to the Elizabethans. Strawberries were also much loved, although the large berries that we are familiar with were unknown until the eighteenth century, when hybrids of two species of American origin were developed. New cultivars of any type of berry – yellow raspberries perhaps, or loganberries (a blackberry–raspberry hybrid) – were enthusiastically taken up by head gardeners eager to extend their range of produce.

Berries of all descriptions are a wonderful basis for crumbles. The smell of hot sugary fruit and buttery crust is divine. They are also lovely for cobblers, producing lots of juice to contrast with the scone-like topping. Strawberries, raspberries, redcurrants and blackcurrants all mix well together and with other fruit. Berries are especially nice combined with vanilla or almond flavours. Experiment to find your favourite combinations.

Savoury Crumbles

Cauliflower Cheese with Parmesan Crumble

A dish for lovers of cheese. Serve as a main course, accompanied by some good bread and a salad.

1 cauliflower
30g butter
30g plain flour
450ml milk
250g mature cheddar, grated

FOR THE PARMESAN CRUMBLE
60g plain flour
60g butter, cut into small cubes
60g Parmesan, finely grated

Boil or steam the cauliflower until just cooked. Drain well, cut into pieces and put into an ovenproof serving dish.

Melt the butter in a large saucepan. Stir in the flour to make a roux, then add the milk a little at a time, stirring to make a smooth sauce. Simmer for a few minutes, then add the cheese and continue to cook, stirring all the time, until the cheese has melted. Pour over the cauliflower.

Preheat the oven to 210°C.

To make the Parmesan crumble, put the flour, butter and Parmesan in a food processor and pulse until the mixture resembles fine breadcrumbs, or rub together by hand. Scatter the mixture over the cauliflower cheese and then splash with a small amount of water – a couple of teaspoons, no more – off the ends of your fingers so that the mixture clumps a little on top. This helps to make the finished texture more interesting.

Put the dish on an oven tray and bake for about 15 minutes, until the sauce is bubbling and the crumble pale gold with darker spots. Serve immediately.

You can prepare the cauliflower cheese and the crumble topping in advance, but add the topping immediately before baking and cook at a slightly lower temperature for a little longer.

Devilled Crab with Parmesan Crumb Topping

Devilled crab is the sort of dish that was enjoyed as a savoury: a piquant, rich mouthful served at the end of Edwardian dinners. It makes a good light lunch or supper, or a rich starter as part of a larger meal.

15g butter
30g shallot or spring onion, very finely chopped
200g prepared crabmeat (brown, or white and brown mixed)
1 teaspoon Worcestershire sauce
1 teaspoon whole grain mustard
½–1 teaspoon very finely chopped fresh red chilli
1 teaspoon grated fresh ginger
15g (2 heaped tablespoons) soft fresh white breadcrumbs
150ml double cream

FOR THE TOPPING
30g self-raising flour
15g butter, cut into small cubes
15g Parmesan, finely grated
30g soft fresh white breadcrumbs

Preheat the oven to 170°C.

Melt the butter in a small frying pan. Add the shallot or spring onion and soften gently without browning. Stir in all the other ingredients, except those for the topping, heat through gently and then divide between four ramekin dishes.

To make the topping, put all the ingredients in a bowl and rub together until you can no longer see the butter. Cover the crab mixture with the topping.

Bake for about 15 minutes or until the filling is piping hot and the top lightly browned and crisp. Leave to cool a little before serving.

Fish with Cheddar and Dill Crumble

Use mature cheddar for this recipe. Dried dill can be used if fresh is unobtainable, but reduce the amount from 1 tablespoon to a scant teaspoon.

30g butter
2 echalion (banana) shallots,
    finely chopped
About 200g spinach, washed and
    roughly chopped
30g plain flour
300ml milk
2 tablespoons crème fraîche
Finely grated zest and juice of
    1 lemon
1 tablespoon chopped fresh dill
1 tablespoon chopped fresh parsley
Salt, pepper, and grated nutmeg
About 700g cod or hake fillet, cut into
    neat slices

FOR THE TOPPING
150g plain flour
50g dry white breadcrumbs
80g mature cheddar, finely grated
1 tablespoon chopped fresh dill
80g butter, melted and cooled but still
    liquid

Preheat the oven to 190°C.

Melt the butter in a large saucepan and cook the shallots gently until soft. Add the spinach and press it down with a wooden spoon until it wilts. Stir well, then stir in the flour. Add the milk and keep stirring over the heat until the mixture thickens. Cook for a little longer, then stir in the crème fraîche, lemon zest and juice, dill and parsley, and season to taste with salt, pepper and a little grated nutmeg. Put the fish into a gratin dish and pour the sauce over.

To make the topping, combine the flour, breadcrumbs, cheese and dill. Pour in the butter, stirring constantly to make a lumpy mixture. Scatter this over the sauce and fish. Bake for 25–30 minutes, until the topping is gold and the fish fully cooked. Serve immediately.

Making Savoury Crumbles

The contrast of crisp topping with soft filling is integral to the definition of a good crumble. As far as proportions are concerned, savoury crumbles tend to taste better with relatively thin, crunchy layers of crumble, closer to a gratin than a pudding. Vegetables, especially summer ones such as courgettes and tomatoes, and fish make lovely crumbles but the texture of meat, including mince, does harmonise especially well with the toppings.

Naturally, the first rule of making a savoury crumble topping is to omit the sugar. Cheese is the usual replacement for sweetness. Parmesan is very successful, relatively small amounts adding concentrated flavour; or try a good mature farmhouse cheddar, finely grated. For savoury fillings in which the vegetables have some natural sweetness, pecorino is a good choice.

Breadcrumbs are another good addition, enhancing the texture of savoury crumbles. Use them to replace a proportion of the flour. They can be soft crumbs from a fresh loaf, or dry ones made by baking stale bread in a low oven and crushing them. Japanese panko breadcrumbs, available from some supermarkets, are good too, but avoid the dried orange breadcrumbs sometimes used for breading ham or coating fish.

Spice flavours often seem to get lost among the butter and cheese. Mustard powder is worth trying, and cayenne pepper adds a piquant note. Some herbs work well, notably thyme, marjoram or dill. Seeds, especially toasted sesame, and nuts, such as almonds or pine nuts, scattered over the top to toast during cooking add flavour and will look attractive.

Leek, Stilton and Walnut Crumble

Good alone as a vegetarian lunch or light supper, or as a side dish with meat or fish.

500–600g floury potatoes, peeled
400–500g leeks (trimmed weight),
   washed and finely sliced
2 cloves garlic, finely sliced
300ml single cream
2 teaspoons cornflour
1 tablespoon finely chopped
   fresh tarragon
4 tablespoons finely chopped
   fresh parsley

Finely grated zest and juice of
   1 lemon (preferably unwaxed)
Salt and pepper
FOR THE TOPPING
120g plain flour
60g butter, cut into cubes
60g blue Stilton
40g walnuts, roughly chopped

Preheat the oven to 200°C.

Cut the potatoes into roughly 1cm cubes. Put them into a saucepan, add water to just cover, bring to the boil and cook for about 8 minutes. Add the leeks and cook for another 2–3 minutes, then drain, reserving the cooking water and leaving the vegetables in the pan. Stir the sliced garlic into the mixture.

Mix the cream and cornflour together and stir into the vegetables. Heat gently, stirring well, until the cream comes to the boil. Thin with a little of the cooking water. Turn off the heat, add the tarragon, parsley and lemon zest, and season with salt, pepper and lemon juice. The mixture should be quite highly seasoned. Tip into a baking dish.

To make the topping, add a pinch of salt to the flour and rub in the butter. Crumble in the Stilton and stir in the walnuts. Spread over the vegetables and bake for 25–30 minutes or until the top is golden and the filling bubbling.

Courgette Crumble

If you grow courgettes you'll know that you can never have enough courgette recipes. This makes a good light lunch or supper, accompanied by salad, or as a side dish for fish.

450–500g courgettes, washed
   and trimmed
1 tablespoon olive oil
2 cloves garlic, crushed
1 onion, finely chopped
150g garlic and herb Boursin cheese

FOR THE TOPPING
80g Emmenthal cheese,
   coarsely grated
60g fresh white breadcrumbs
60g plain flour
Pinch of salt
40g butter, melted and cooled
   but still liquid

Preheat the oven to 170°C.

Halve the courgettes lengthways (or quarter them if they are large), then cut into slices about 5mm thick. Put the oil, courgettes, garlic and onion into a frying pan and cook gently, stirring frequently. Once the onions are translucent and the courgettes soft, add the Boursin, broken up into several pieces, stir well to mix, and then transfer the mixture to a baking dish.

To make the topping, put the Emmenthal, breadcrumbs, flour and salt into a bowl. Drizzle in the butter, stirring vigorously to make an uneven crumbly mixture. Spoon over the courgette mixture. Bake for 20–25 minutes and serve hot.

Vegetables

A huge range of vegetables were grown in the walled kitchen gardens of big houses. To get an idea of what was available, visit Tatton Park (Cheshire) to see a garden entirely planted with varieties developed in the nineteenth century. The highly accomplished chefs who worked in some of these houses almost certainly used them in gratins – cooked vegetables under a rich sauce, topped with breadcrumbs and cheese and grilled. Crumbles were unknown to them, but a cheese-rich savoury version is excellent with some vegetables.

Pumpkins and squash were grown mostly for entertainment value in the past, valued for their ornamental appearance rather than for eating. There was much more enthusiasm for the botanically related cucumbers and melons. For such crops, special 'hot beds' were constructed, such those still made at Acorn Bank (Cumbria), in which deep layers of decaying farmyard manure provide warmth for the roots of tender plants. Marrows have been widely grown in gardens since the nineteenth century, but their smaller relatives, courgettes, do not seem to have been popular until the 1960s.

Pumpkins and tomatoes both make good crumble bases. American-style pumpkin pies or muffins respond well to sweet crumble toppings. Slindon (Sussex) holds a mid-autumn pumpkin festival of these visually stunning fruit – for technically they are the fruit of the plant, complete with seeds.

Tomatoes, of course, are also fruit, even though usually treated as vegetables. They make interesting savoury crumbles, but they must be really good late-summer tomatoes with firm, beefy flesh, not pallid watery winter offerings. To taste a range and find out more, visit the Wimpole Tomato Festival where the fabulous kitchen garden of this great house in Cambridgeshire celebrates them every September; or try Knightshayes in Devon, to view their collection of over 100 heritage varieties.

Tomato and Aubergine Crumble

Make this with late summer tomatoes, choosing large, firm-fleshed varieties such as coeur de boeuf or plum tomatoes, or visit Wimpole Tomato Festival (Cambridgeshire) for more inspiration.

2 aubergines
6–8 tablespoons olive oil
About 800g tomatoes
2 echalion (banana) shallots, chopped
1 clove garlic, crushed
½ teaspoon salt
1 teaspoon muscovado sugar
Small bunch basil, leaves only
Small bunch parsley, leaves only

FOR THE TOPPING
80g plain flour
80g fresh white breadcrumbs
40g mature pecorino cheese,
    finely grated
80g butter, melted and cooled but
    still liquid
2 tablespoons pine nuts

Preheat the oven to 180°C.

Cut the aubergines into slices about 1cm thick and brush both sides lightly with olive oil. Grill under a high heat for about 3–5 minutes on each side, or until beginning to soften, then leave to cool.

Add a tablespoon of the oil to a frying pan and cook the shallots and garlic gently for about 5 minutes. Drop the tomatoes in boiling water for 15 seconds, remove and peel off the skins. Slice thickly.

Blend the remaining olive oil with the salt, sugar, basil and parsley to make a thick paste.

Put half of the shallot mixture into a baking dish, then add half the aubergine slices and half of the tomatoes. Repeat. Pour the herb and oil mixture over.

To make the topping, mix the flour, breadcrumbs and cheese, then stir in the butter to give a crumbly texture, and spoon over the vegetables. Scatter the pine nuts over. Bake for 20–30 minutes, until the top is golden and the filling bubbling.

Eat warm or just cooled, as a light lunch or supper, or as an accompaniment to grilled meat.

Savoury Cobblers

Chestnut and Mushroom Cobbler

A hearty, filling, winter vegetarian dish. It can be made vegan by replacing the butter in the topping with vegetable fat; be sure to check that the other ingredients are vegan too.

2 tablespoons neutral-flavoured oil, such as sunflower
1 onion, finely chopped
2 sticks celery, finely chopped
2 cloves garlic, crushed
400g chestnut mushrooms, sliced
About 350–380g cooked peeled chestnuts
2–3 tbsp red wine or port
500ml vegetable stock
1 piece star anise
2 strips orange zest
1 tablespoon cornflour slaked in a little cold water
Salt and pepper

FOR THE TOPPING
225g self-raising flour, plus extra for dusting
2 teaspoons mustard powder
75g butter, chilled
About 75ml milk or water
Cream or beaten egg to glaze (optional)

Preheat the oven to 190°C.

Heat the oil in a large frying pan. Add the onion, celery and garlic and fry gently until soft and translucent. Stir in the sliced mushrooms and cook for another 5–10 minutes, until they are soft.

Add the chestnuts and the wine or port and cook for a minute longer, then stir in the stock, star anise and orange zest. Bring to the boil, reduce the heat and simmer gently for a few minutes. Add the cornflour and water and stir until the sauce is transparent. Season to taste with salt and pepper, then pour into a shallow baking dish.

To make the topping, mix the flour and mustard powder, and a scant teaspoon of salt. Grate in the butter and stir just enough to distribute it through the flour. Add 75ml water or milk and mix to a soft dough. A little more liquid may be needed. On a floured work surface, roll out the dough to about 2cm thick and cut out round scones using a biscuit cutter. Gather the scraps and re-roll to cut out more rounds. Arrange the rounds over the chestnut mixture, brush with cream or egg if desired, and bake for 15–20 minutes until golden brown.

Serve with Brussels sprouts, green beans or a salad.

Vegetable Cobbler

A recipe by Sarah Edington, from her *Classic British Cooking*.

3 medium carrots, peeled and sliced
½ a small cauliflower, separated
  into florets
75g butter
8 small leeks, thickly sliced
2 small heads of fennel, halved and
  sliced across
25g wholemeal flour
425ml vegetable stock
Salt and pepper
2 tablespoons chopped fresh parsley

FOR THE TOPPING
225g self-raising flour, plus extra
  for dusting
1 teaspoon mixed herbs
1 teaspoon mustard powder
50g vegetarian lard, cut into cubes
1 egg, beaten
Milk to mix
2 tablespoons chopped fresh parsley
75g mature cheddar, grated

Preheat the oven to 180°C.

Boil the carrots and cauliflower for 5 minutes. Drain and place in a baking dish. Melt half the butter in a frying pan and fry the leeks and fennel over a moderate heat for 3–4 minutes. Add to the dish. Melt the rest of the butter in a small pan, add the flour and cook gently for a few minutes. Gradually add the vegetable stock. Taste and adjust the seasoning. Simmer for a minute or two, then add the parsley and pour over the vegetables. Cover and bake for 30 minutes.

To make the topping, sift the flour with the mixed herbs, mustard powder, ½ teaspoon salt and a little pepper. Rub in the lard until the mixture resembles coarse breadcrumbs. Mix the egg with a little milk and combine with the flour mix to make a dough. On a floured work surface, roll out to about 2cm thick and cut out round scones using a biscuit cutter. Arrange on top of the vegetables and sprinkle with the grated cheese. Turn the oven up to 230°C and bake for a further 15 minutes until pale gold.

Making Savoury Cobblers

Cobbler doughs have a fairly neutral flavour; sugar isn't essential and can easily be omitted. This, and the texture of the soft biscuit dough, which is fluffier and akin to bread, means that cobblers work well with savoury fillings.

As with sweet cobblers, variety comes partly through the fats used. Cooks in the deep south of the USA would have used lard as a fat for biscuit making (including sweet ones – not so alien when one thinks of the British tradition of using lard to mix the shortest of shortcrust pastries for both sweet and savoury pies). To add character, try butter, cream, sour cream, or a little olive oil in place of some dairy fat. Some cobbler toppings are really dumpling doughs, which suggests trying beef suet for a British variation.

The softer dough of cobbler toppings picks up savoury seasonings better than crumbles do. Mustard, cayenne and herbs such as chives, thyme and marjoram work well, or add some grated cheddar.

Cobblers are more visually interesting than crumbles. Feeling neat and tidy? Roll out a standard dough, cut it in rounds, and arrange in overlapping layers across the top, or as a necklace around the edge of the dish. In a hurry? Divide the dough and shape the pieces roughly by hand. They can be patchworked over the filling for a rustic topping. Try glazing the dough with cream or beaten egg and add a sprinkling of grated cheese.

Cobblers can be reheated but never have quite the same freshness and lightness as they do when first baked, so do aim to eat them on the day of baking. Meat- or vegetable-based fillings are always eaten hot.

Turkey and Ham Cobbler

Good for using Christmas leftovers. Chicken or meat from game birds can be used instead, and leftover vegetables (peas, green beans, leeks, celery, chestnuts, mushrooms) are all good additions.

50g butter
50g plain flour
600ml turkey or chicken stock
  (make up the quantity with milk
  if necessary)
Salt, pepper
350–400g cooked turkey, cut into
  1cm dice
150–200g cooked ham, cut into 1cm
  dice
200–300g leftover cooked vegetables
  (optional), cut into neat pieces

FOR THE TOPPING
350g self-raising flour, plus extra
  for dusting
Finely grated zest of
  1 unwaxed lemon
Leaves from 6–8 good sprigs of
  thyme, or 1 teaspoon dried thyme
150g butter, chilled
About 8 tablespoons milk or water
Beaten egg or cream to glaze

Preheat the oven to 190°C.

Melt the butter in a large saucepan. Stir in the flour to make a roux, then add the stock a little at a time, stirring to make a smooth sauce. Simmer for a few minutes and season with salt and pepper. Add the meat and the vegetables if using. Stir well and heat through thoroughly. Pour into a baking dish.

To make the topping, put the flour in a bowl; stir in the lemon zest, thyme, and a teaspoon of salt. Grate in the butter and mix it through the flour. Add the milk or water and stir well to make a soft dough. On a floured work surface, roll out the dough to about 1cm thick and cut out 7cm rounds. Gather the scraps and re-roll to cut out more rounds. Overlap the rounds to cover the turkey and ham mixture and brush with beaten egg or cream. Put the dish on an oven tray and bake for about 30 minutes or until the top is cooked and golden and the sauce bubbling.

Serve with a salad or extra vegetables.

Winter Beef Cobbler

An update of the stew and dumplings that simmered in ranges throughout Britain, from Lake District farmhouses to the Birmingham back-to-backs (when the inhabitants could afford meat). If you don't want to use lard or beef suet, substitute oil and butter or vegetable suet.

30g lard
1 onion, chopped
1 clove garlic, crushed
1 stick celery, chopped
400g stewing beef, cubed
30g plain flour
About 400g (prepared weight) turnips, carrots and parsnips, cut into chunks
450ml beef stock or beer (not too bitter)
Salt and pepper

FOR THE TOPPING
250g self-raising flour, plus extra for dusting
125g suet
1 teaspoon salt
1 tablespoon chopped fresh herbs (rosemary, marjoram, thyme) or 2 teaspoons mustard powder
About 200ml milk or water

Preheat the oven to 140°C.

Melt the lard in a frying pan and add the onion, garlic and celery. Fry gently until translucent, then remove and set aside.

Toss the meat into flour and fry, turning until brown on all sides. Return the onion mixture to the pan and add the vegetables, turning well. Sprinkle in any remaining flour and stir in the stock or beer. Bring to a simmer and season with a scant teaspoon of salt and a dusting of pepper. Transfer to a casserole dish and cook for at least 2 hours, until the meat is tender. Taste and adjust the seasoning if necessary. The stew can be made in advance and reheated.

When ready to add the topping, set the oven to 220°C and put the stew in to heat.

Mix the flour, suet, salt and herbs or mustard, then add the milk or water and mix to make a soft, slightly sticky dough. On a floured work surface, roll out the dough to about 1cm thick and cut out 7cm rounds. Use these to cover the surface of the hot stew and return to the oven for 15–20 minutes or until cooked.

Serve immediately; this is a meal in itself but add broccoli, cabbage or Brussels sprouts on the side, if liked.

Cobbler History

Cobblers are firmly associated with North America and are deep-dish pies with a thick topping of southern-style biscuit dough. To British tastes this seems like a scone – although American soft biscuits are lighter and often less sweet than scones.

The origin of the name is mysterious but the cobbler may have got its name because the surface, with dough formed roughly into dumplings or cut more neatly into rounds, resembles cobblestones. Alternatively, it could be because it was 'cobbled together' using whatever fruit was available and a simple and quickly mixed dough. Either way, cobblers share with crumbles a note of expediency and improvisation, and take their place in gastronomy as unfussy and informal dishes.

Cobblers have a longer history than crumbles, dating back to the mid-nineteenth century, although their genesis is uncertain. They may have been improvised versions of pies, using a dough that requires less fat than pastry. Or they could be the inheritors of a stew and dumpling tradition. A sweet cobbler could be viewed as a fruit stew with dumplings. Some seem simply to be deep-dish pies with top and bottom crusts. Others, with whimsical names such as slumps or grunts, are traditionally cooked on the stove top.

The origins of recipes are rarely clear-cut, but one thing is certain: the development of chemical raising agents such as bicarbonate of soda and baking powder in the 1840s was essential to soft biscuits.

Cobblers seem to have found their way into British cookery books in the late 1960s or early 70s. They were a novelty and caught on despite the British usage of the word 'cobblers' as a vulgar term for rubbish. In Britain, savoury versions have always been as popular as sweet versions, possibly more so, since the combination of a meaty stew and a bready topping is attuned to British tastes.

Haddock and Prawn Cobbler

This is a recipe that originated in the National Trust tea room at the Treasurer's House in York. It uses a scone-type topping.

700g haddock fillet, skinned and cut
    into 5cm chunks
50g butter
50g plain flour
2 teaspoons mustard powder
600ml milk
4 teaspoons wine vinegar
Salt, pepper
50g prawns
2 hard-boiled eggs, peeled
    and chopped

FOR THE TOPPING
175g wholemeal flour, plus extra
    for dusting
1 tablespoon baking powder
Pinch of dried thyme
40g butter, cut into cubes
1 egg, beaten
2 tablespoons milk, plus extra
    to glaze

Preheat the oven to 180°C.

Cook the haddock in simmering water for about 10 minutes. Leave to cool. Melt the butter, stir in the flour and mustard powder, and then the milk and wine vinegar. If it curdles, whisk well. Season to taste with salt and pepper. Lay the cooked haddock in a baking dish. Scatter on the prawns and hard-boiled eggs and pour the sauce over.

To make the topping, sift the flour, baking powder and thyme into a large bowl. Rub in the butter, then add the egg and milk and mix to make a dough. On a floured work surface, roll out to about 1cm thick. Cut out 2cm rounds and arrange over the fish mixture. Brush with milk and bake for about 20 minutes, until well risen and brown.

Serve with vegetables or green salad.

Minced Lamb with Potato Scone Cobbler

This recipe uses a potato scone mix made with olive oil. A neutral-flavoured oil such as sunflower or rapeseed can be used instead, or substitute melted butter if you prefer.

1 tablespoon olive oil
1 clove garlic, crushed
1 small onion, finely chopped
500g minced lamb
Generous pinch of ground cumin
About 60ml red wine
1 tablespoon tomato purée
1 tablespoon chopped fresh oregano
    leaves, or 1 teaspoon dried
About 200ml chicken, lamb or
    beef stock
Salt and pepper

FOR THE TOPPING
450g floury potatoes
6 spring onions, chopped
100ml olive oil
250g self-raising flour, plus extra for
    dusting
About 100ml milk

Preheat the oven to 200°C.

Heat the oil in a frying pan and cook the garlic and onion gently until translucent. Add the mince, using the back of a spoon to break it up, and turn up the heat to brown it. Stir in the cumin and cook for a few minutes longer, then add the wine and let it bubble. Stir in the tomato purée, oregano, stock, a teaspoon of salt and some pepper. Bring to the boil, then reduce the heat and simmer gently for at least 1 hour. Tip into a baking dish. Cover and keep hot in the oven (or leave to cool and then reheat just before adding the topping).

To make the topping, peel the potatoes, cut into chunks and boil until tender.

Drain thoroughly, then mash, preferably by passing them through a potato ricer or vegetable mill. Weigh out 250g (reserve the remainder for another recipe). Add the spring onions, then the olive oil and a teaspoon of salt. Stir in the flour and add the milk to make a soft mixture. Dust a work surface with flour and form the mixture into a roll about 5cm in diameter. Cut into 1cm slices and use these, slightly overlapping, to cover the lamb. Bake for about 30 minutes, until the topping is well risen and golden.

Chicken Cobbler

This topping is based on North American buttermilk biscuits. They need a very hot oven for the initial cooking.

1 tablespoon olive oil
50g unsmoked pancetta, cubed
1 small onion, finely chopped
1 clove garlic, crushed
2 sticks celery, finely chopped
About 500g chicken, cut into 1cm dice
100ml white wine
30g plain flour
300ml chicken stock
Salt and pepper
About 300g cooked vegetables –
    peas, mangetout, green beans
    or asparagus

FOR THE TOPPING
250g plain flour, plus extra for dusting
4 teaspoons baking powder
¾ teaspoon salt
60g butter, cut into small cubes
2 teaspoons finely chopped
    fresh tarragon
About 200ml buttermilk

Preheat the oven to 230°C.

Heat the oil in a frying pan, add the pancetta and cook gently until the fat runs. Add the onion, garlic and celery and fry until translucent. Add the chicken and cook, stirring frequently, for about 5 minutes. Pour in the wine and let it bubble, then shake over the flour. Stir in the stock, bring to the boil and simmer gently for about 15 minutes or until the meat is cooked through.

Add the cooked vegetables, season to taste with salt and pepper and pour into a baking dish.

To make the topping, put the flour, baking powder, salt and butter in a food processor and pulse until the mix resembles fine breadcrumbs.

(Alternatively, the butter can be rubbed in by hand, but handle as lightly as possible.) Tip into a bowl, add the tarragon and buttermilk and mix with a knife just enough to make a sticky dough. On a floured surface, pat out to about 2cm thick and cut out 5cm rounds, gathering and re-rolling the scraps. Place the rounds so they touch but don't overlap on top of the chicken and bake for 10 minutes.

Turn the oven down to 150°C and cook for another 15 minutes, or until the meat is thoroughly hot and the topping cooked through.

Creative Crumbles

Vanilla Ice Cream with Ginger Crumble and Rhubarb

A rich combination for a special dessert. Vanilla pannacotta or creamy Greek yoghurt are good alternatives to ice cream.

About 400g forced rhubarb
   (trimmed weight)
50g sugar (any type)
1 quantity Vanilla Ice Cream
   (page 120)
4 pieces stem ginger in syrup, drained
   and chopped into small dice

FOR THE GINGER CRUMBLE
50g plain flour
50g porridge oats
50g soft pale brown or golden caster
   sugar
½ teaspoon ground ginger
50g butter, melted and cooled but still
   liquid

Preheat the oven to 180°C.

Cut the rhubarb into 1–2cm lengths and put them into a baking dish in which they fit in one layer. Sprinkle the sugar over, cover with foil and bake for 15 minutes. Uncover and cook for another 15 minutes or until soft. Leave to cool.

While the rhubarb cooks, make the ginger crumble: mix the flour, oats, sugar and ground ginger, then drizzle in the butter, stirring to give a lumpy consistency. Spread the mixture on an oven tray and bake alongside the rhubarb for 15–20 minutes. Stir once or twice so it cooks evenly. Leave to cool and break up any large pieces.

If the ice cream is frozen hard, remove from the freezer and leave at room temperature for 20 minutes. Divide between six serving dishes, rippling the rhubarb and stem ginger through the mixture. Top with a portion of crumble.

Rhubarb

The best place to view (and sometimes taste) rhubarb is at Clumber Park in Nottinghamshire. It's home to the National Collection of Rhubarb, over 130 varieties are grown here (the second largest collection in the world), and a Rhubarb Month celebrates the plant. Rhubarb became something of an English speciality in the nineteenth century. It is a plant that likes heavy clay soil and plenty of nutrients, and requires several weeks of winter cold to flourish – conditions that parts of Britain provide very well. These were especially apparent near Nostell in West Yorkshire; it lies on the edge of the Rhubarb Triangle, so-called because of the cultivation of the plant as a commercial crop there. The shocking pink stems of rhubarb that appear on the market around Christmas are produced by a special system. This uses heated sheds for the final cropping: the rhubarb crowns are packed in in total darkness and kept in a warm atmosphere. They begin to grow, producing slender shoots with a delicate flavour and startling colour, topped off by the buds of bright yellow-green leaves. The only light allowed is candle light, used when harvesting the rhubarb.

The principle of forcing in the dark was developed by gardeners in the kitchen gardens of large houses. They used large ornamental terracotta pots to cover the rhubarb crowns. These had removable lids that allowed the gardeners to harvest the slender coloured stems in early spring. Outdoor-grown rhubarb is a different item, stronger in taste, coarser in texture and greener in colour. If using this, try to choose small, slender stems.

Rhubarb is the fleshy stem of the plant and so is not technically a fruit, but it is treated as one in the British kitchen. Sharply acidic, the filling will need some sugar even before it goes under a sweet crumble topping. Vanilla, orange and ginger combine well with rhubarb and it is good with summer berries such as strawberries and raspberries – they lend it a fruity sweetness while it provides a tangy sharpness.

Crème Fraîche Ice Cream with Blueberries and Almond Crumble

This ice cream is very simple to make. Any leftover is good with other crumbles.

FOR THE CRÈME FRAÎCHE ICE CREAM
150g icing sugar
150ml whole milk
A little vanilla essence or paste
450g crème fraîche

FOR THE BLUEBERRY SAUCE
200g blueberries, washed
200g granulated sugar

FOR THE ALMOND CRUMBLE
60g plain flour
60g granulated sugar
40g butter
1 teaspoon honey or golden syrup
1 drop almond essence
25g blanched almonds, very
  roughly chopped

To make the ice cream, whisk the icing sugar, milk and vanilla together until the sugar has dissolved, then whisk in the crème fraîche. Churn in an ice-cream maker according to the manufacturer's instructions or freeze and stir according to the method given for Vanilla Ice Cream (page 136).

To make the blueberry sauce, put the blueberries and sugar in a pan with 2 tablespoons water and stir over a gentle heat for about 10 minutes, until the berries have collapsed to make a thick sauce. Leave to cool, then chill.

Preheat the oven to 180°C.

To make the almond crumble, mix the flour and sugar. Melt the butter over a low heat and add the almond essence and honey or golden syrup. Stir into the flour mixture to give a lumpy consistency and add the almonds. Spread in a thin layer on an oven tray and bake for 15–20 minutes. Stir once or twice during baking. Leave to cool and break up any large pieces.

If the ice cream is frozen hard, remove from the freezer and leave at room temperature for 20 minutes. Divide between six serving dishes, rippling the blueberry sauce through the mixture. Top with a portion of crumble.

Honey Ice Cream with Pears and Pecan Crumble

A simple and unusual ice cream. Bee conservation is an important part of the National Trust's work. Visit Attingham Park (Shropshire) to view the Grade II-listed Georgian bee house, or Sissinghurst (Kent) where the bees feed on the apple blossom in the orchard.

600ml double cream
200g honey
150ml whole milk
2 teaspoons lemon juice
A little vanilla essence or paste
FOR THE PEARS
6 small cooking pears, peeled, quartered and cored
Juice of ½ a lemon
2 teaspoons butter
30g vanilla sugar

FOR THE PECAN CRUMBLE
80g plain flour
60g soft pale brown sugar
½ teaspoon ground cinnamon
25g pecans, coarsely chopped
60g butter, melted and cooled but still liquid

To make the ice cream, mix all the ingredients and churn in an ice-cream maker according to the manufacturer's instructions. Transfer to a plastic container and put in the freezer for about 60 minutes, until firm. If you don't have an ice-cream maker, freeze and stir according to the method given for Vanilla Ice Cream (page 136).

Preheat the oven to 180°C.

For the pears, put the fruit into a shallow baking dish. Add the lemon juice, butter, vanilla sugar and about 2 tablespoons water. Cover and bake for 25 minutes, or until soft. Leave to cool to tepid.

To make the pecan crumble, mix the flour, brown sugar, cinnamon and chopped pecans. Stir in the melted butter. Spread the mixture on an oven tray and bake for 15–20 minutes. Stir once or twice during cooking. Leave to cool and break up any large pieces.

To serve, divide the pears between six dishes. Add a scoop or two of ice cream and scatter the crumble over.

Peach Crumble Cheesecake

A rich and delicious baked cheesecake. If decent fresh peaches are not available, use sliced ones canned in juice.

FOR THE CRUMBLE CRUST AND TOPPING
100g plain flour
75g digestive biscuits, crushed
30g demerara sugar
½ teaspoon grated nutmeg
½ teaspoon ground cinnamon
75g butter, melted and cooled but
   still liquid

FOR THE FILLING
130g caster sugar
2 eggs
A few drops vanilla essence
500g cream cheese, softened
250g peaches, skinned and sliced

Preheat the oven to 180°C.

Butter a deep 20 cm diameter cake tin with a removable base.

To make the crumble, mix the flour, crushed biscuits, demerara sugar, nutmeg and cinnamon. Drizzle in the butter, stirring with a fork to make a lumpy dough. Take two thirds of this and spread it over the base of the tin in a thin, even layer. Bake for 8–10 minutes, then leave to cool. Chill the remaining mixture.

To make the filling, put the caster sugar, eggs and vanilla essence in a bowl and whisk until very thick and pale. Work the cream cheese with a wooden spoon until smooth, then stir into the sugar and egg mixture and mix well. Spoon about a quarter of this over the cooled base, then spread the sliced peaches over. Pour in the rest of the cream cheese mixture and give the tin a gentle shake to make sure everything is level.

Take the remaining crumble mixture and work it between your fingers to make sure it is crumbly. Carefully add this to the top of the cake, sprinkling it around the edge in a 2–3cm wide band, leaving the middle clear.

Bake for 40 minutes, then turn the oven off and leave the cheesecake in the oven for another hour. Remove from the oven, leave to cool, and chill thoroughly before serving.

COOKING TIP: To skin fresh peaches, lower them into boiling water for about 30 seconds. Remove and the skins should slip off easily.

White Chocolate and Gooseberry Crumble Upside-Down Cheesecake

An elegant pale green and cream filling, with a rich, decadent texture. Make it the day before it's needed. Temperature is important when mixing.

500g gooseberries, topped and tailed
Sugar to taste
FOR THE CRUMBLE TOPPING
120g plain flour
60g granulated sugar
60g butter, cut into cubes

FOR THE CHEESECAKE
200g white chocolate, chopped
200g ricotta, at room temperature
200g mascarpone, at room temperature
200ml double cream, chilled

Put the gooseberries in a pan with about 3 tablespoons water and place over a low heat. Cook gently until the berries are soft, but try not to let them collapse completely. Sweeten to taste and leave to cool.

Preheat the oven to 180°C.

Lightly oil a deep 20 cm diameter cake tin with a removable base and line with baking paper.

To make the crumble, mix the flour and sugar and rub in the butter. Spread the mixture on an oven tray and bake for 15–20 minutes, until pale gold. Stir once or twice during cooking. Leave to cool completely.

To make the cheesecake, melt the white chocolate in a bowl over a pan of barely simmering water, stirring frequently until all is melted, and then put it aside until tepid (but don't let it set).

Drain any liquid off the ricotta and beat together with the mascarpone. Whip the cream until it forms soft peaks and fold into the cheese mixture. Quickly stir in the melted chocolate, mixing well. Leaving behind as much liquid as possible, stir the gooseberries through the mixture – aim for a marbled effect rather than a completely even mix. Pour this over the base of the tin. Top with the crumble, pressing it down very lightly.

Chill for at least 6 hours or preferably overnight. Remove from the tin before serving.

Pear and Hazelnut Mug Crumble

In a hurry? Want crumble now? Just enough for one person?
Christelle Huet-Gomez spotted a need and wrote her book *Mug
Crumbles* in response. If there aren't enough recipes in there, here
are a couple more. You will need a large mug and a microwave.

15g skinned hazelnuts (in practice,
 this is 15 nuts)

2 heaped tablespoons plain flour

2 tablespoons soft brown sugar (a bit
 less if the pear is really ripe)

Pinch of salt

15g butter (1 slice of butter 5mm
 thick off a 250g block)

1 small Conference pear, peeled,
 cored and cut in small chunks

First toast the hazelnuts: put them on a microwaveable plate and cook
on high for 2 minutes. Stir, then cook again at 1 minute intervals,
stirring between each burst, for a total of about 5 minutes or until
gold. Use oven gloves to remove the plate, which will get hot. Leave
to cool, then chop or crush coarsely.

Mix the flour, half the sugar and a tiny pinch of salt, then rub in
the butter until the mixture resembles breadcrumbs. Stir in the
chopped nuts.

Put the pear chunks in the mug. Cover with cling film, pierce several
holes in the top and microwave on 800W for 1 minute. Pour off the
excess juice and heat for another 30 seconds. Add the remaining
sugar and top with the crumble mix. Heat on 800W for 1 minute 30
seconds, leave to cool a little and enjoy.

This recipe can be baked conventionally if wished, using large
ramekins (6–7cm diameter). Put the pear and sugar in a ramekin, add
the crumble and bake in a preheated oven at 190°C for 10–15 minutes.
Scale up by multiplying all ingredients by the number of people present.

Blackberries

Of all fruit, blackberries can be the cheapest: all they cost is the effort taken to gather them. The canes root in the most unpromising locations, in corners of waste ground and along walls or fences even in urban locations. In the countryside they are abundant in late summer hedgerows and on the edge of woodlands. In some areas the National Trust lists walks that are good for blackberry picking.

Blackberries are easy to forage. They are a good fruit for children to collect, obvious and easy to pick (but the best are always just out of reach – watch out for the spines on the brambles and the nettles growing among them!). They are also relatively large and a satisfying quantity can be gathered in a short space of time. Go for them towards the end of August and in September. Blackberries become mushy and tasteless as the nights draw in and temperatures cool. The end of the season is traditionally Michaelmas Day (29th September) when, according to country tradition, 'the Devil spits on them'. After this they are worthless.

As an ingredient they work well on their own, or in the classic combination of blackberry and apple. A good tip here comes from the late Jane Grigson, a champion of traditional British food: instead of cooking apples such as Bramleys, try using dual-purpose apples of the pippin type, such as Blenheim Orange, which offer more flavour and texture. Alternatively, try a combination of pear and blackberry, or experiment by combining them with other berries to give juicy, richly flavoured mixes.

Blackberry, Mascarpone and Amaretti Mug Crumble

Creamy, almondy, with juicy autumn berries. You will need a large mug and a microwave.

30g (2 tablespoons) mascarpone

½ the mug's capacity of blackberries (about 75g)

2 teaspoons caster sugar (8–10g), preferably vanilla sugar

2 heaped tablespoons flour

1 tablespoon soft brown sugar

15g butter (1 slice of butter 5mm thick off a 250g block)

1 tablespoon amaretti crumbs (2 or 3 crisp amaretti, crushed)

Put the mascarpone in the mug. Add the blackberries and the caster sugar.

To make the topping, rub together the flour, brown sugar and butter, using your fingertips, until the mixture resembles breadcrumbs. Stir in the amaretti crumbs. Pile this mixture over the berries. Microwave on 800W for 50 seconds, then leave to cool a little and enjoy.

This recipe can be baked conventionally if wished, using large ramekins (6–7cm diameter). Put the mascarpone, berries and caster sugar in a ramekin, add the crumble and bake in a preheated oven at 190°C for 10–15 minutes. Scale up by multiplying all ingredients by the number of people present.

Proper Egg Custard

From *Recipes from the Dairy* (1998) by Robin Weir and Caroline Liddell with Peter Brears, this is an excellent accompaniment to sweet crumbles and cobblers and the starting point for Vanilla Ice Cream (see page 136).

300ml whole milk
1 vanilla pod, spilt lengthways,
 or 1 teaspoon vanilla paste

100g granulated sugar
3 egg yolks

Put the milk and the vanilla pod and half of the sugar in a saucepan and heat to just below boiling point. Remove from the heat, cover and leave to infuse for at least 15 minutes.

In a heatproof bowl, combine the egg yolks with the remaining sugar. Beat with a hand-held electric mixer until the mixture is thick and pale and holds its shape for a few seconds when a ribbon of mix is trailed across the top. Bring the milk back to boiling point and pour onto the yolks and sugar in a thin stream, whisking steadily.

Place the bowl over a pan of simmering water and stir frequently with a wooden spoon until the custard thickens: judge by looking at the mixture on the back of the spoon. If it forms a thin film, draw a finger across; if this holds when the spoon is tilted, it should be thick enough. (If you have a temperature probe, it should read 85°C). As soon as the required thickness and/or temperature are achieved, remove the pan from the heat, pour the mixture into a jug, remove the vanilla pod and serve.

Vanilla Ice Cream

Proper egg custard forms the base for this very good ice cream; the instructions are based on those given by Robin Weir and Caroline Liddell.

1 quantity Proper Egg Custard
  (page 135)
250ml whipping cream

Make the custard as directed. Leave it to cool and then chill thoroughly.

Remove the vanilla pod, scraping out the little black seeds into the mixture. Add the cream and churn using an ice-cream maker according to the manufacturer's instructions. Transfer to a plastic container and put in the freezer for about 60 minutes, until firm.

If you don't have an ice-cream maker, put the chilled mixture in a plastic container in the freezer. Remove after 1–1½ hours and stir (a brief whisk with a hand-held mixer is the best way). Return to the freezer. Repeat twice, then freeze until solid.

Allow 20 minutes at room temperature to soften before serving.

The Importance of Custard

Sweet crumbles and cobblers need some kind of creamy accompaniment to cut the fruity sweetness and contrast with the crunchy textures. In Britain, until recently, the choice was simple: custard.

Where would British cooks have been without custard powder in the twentieth century? A jug of custard was a standby for all puddings. At its best it is unctuous, vanilla-scented, sweet, primrose-coloured. At its worst, it is lumpy and stodgily thick. However, good or bad, it is always served in liberal quantities, and is still the taste of childhood for many people.

Custard has a venerable history and can claim medieval origins. The powdered version is an invention of the mid-nineteenth century, when Alfred Bird invented it for his wife, who was allergic to eggs.

Proper custard, or crème anglaise (even the French name identifies custard with England) is undoubtedly more difficult to make – incautious heating leads to sweet scrambled egg, or a nasty separated mass of curds if things go really wrong – but when well made it has a lightness and delicacy that custard powder cannot imitate.

Ice cream is especially popular in north America, and what is vanilla ice cream but a frozen egg custard? Admittedly, the grunts, slumps and buckles of New England are sometimes eaten with hard sauces: like brandy butter, these are concoctions of sugar and butter, flavoured with vanilla or rum.

An alternative accompaniment is cream in various forms, from a drizzle of thin pouring cream which deliciously combines with the hot fruit juices, to extra-thick double cream on the side, picking up a little with each spoonful of crumble. Sour cream is excellent with cobblers and crème fraîche goes well with almost any sweet crumble or cobbler. Mascarpone is, on the whole, a little too rich; serve it in small amounts with almondy toppings and stone fruit fillings.

More custard, anyone?

Notes

- All spoon measurements are level, unless specified otherwise.

  1 teaspoon = 5ml
  1 tablespoon = 15ml

- Eggs are medium, unless specified otherwise.

- Oven temperatures are for conventional ovens. If you use a fan oven you may need to reduce the temperature by 10°C.

Index

Acorn Bank, Cumbria
49, 99
almonds: almond and
berry crumble slices 86
crème fraîche ice cream
with blueberries and
almond crumble 122–3
lemon curd crumble
muffins 70–1
plum and amaretti
crumble 22
amaretti: blackberry,
mascarpone and
amaretti mug crumble
132
plum and amaretti
crumble 22
apples 11, 48–9
apple and blackberry
cobbler 30
apple brown betty
17–18
apple cake with
crumble topping 46–7
apple cheesecake
crumble bars 81–2
apple crisp 12
apple pandowdy 40
Dutch apple tart 50–1
never-fail apple
crumble 10
quince, pear and
apple crumble with
marzipan 25–6

apricots 79
apricot and oat crumble
bars 77–8
apricot and pistachio
crumble 21
Ardress House, Co
Armagh 49
Attingham Park,
Shropshire 87
aubergines: tomato and
aubergine crumble
100–1

Barrington Court,
Somerset 48
bars, crumble 77–8,
81–2, 85–6
beef: winter beef cobbler
110–11
Beningbrough, North
Yorks 87
berries: almond and
berry crumble slices 86
berry cobbler with sour
cream biscuits 42–3
bettys 17–19
bilberries 76
blackberries 11, 131
apple and blackberry
cobbler 30
blackberry, mascarpone
and amaretti mug
crumble 132
blackcurrant buckle 36–7

blueberries 76
blueberry muffins with
cinnamon streusel
74–5
blueberry slump 38
crème fraîche ice cream
with blueberries and
almond crumble 122–3
Brockhampton,
Herefordshire 48, 79
buckles 36–7, 39

cakes 44–7, 57–67
Calke, Derbyshire 80
cauliflower cheese with
Parmesan crumble
90–1
cheese: cauliflower
cheese with Parmesan
crumble 90–1
fish with Cheddar and
dill crumble 94–5
leek, Stilton and walnut
crumble 97
cheesecake: apple
cheesecake crumble
bars 81–2
peach crumble
cheesecake 126–7
white chocolate and
gooseberry crumble
upside-down
cheesecake 128–9
chestnut and mushroom

cobbler 104–5
chicken cobbler 116–17
chocolate: chocolate chip
  crumb cake 66–7
  white chocolate and
  gooseberry crumble
  upside-down
  cheesecake 128–9
Christmas mincemeat
  and cranberry crumble
  bars 85
Clumber Park, Notts 49,
  87, 121
cod: fish with Cheddar
  and dill crumble 94–5
containers 23
cooking tips 23–4
Cotehele, Cornwall 49
Coughton Court, Warks
  27, 49
courgette crumble 98
crab: devilled crab with
  Parmesan crumb
  topping 92–3
Cragside,
  Northumberland 80
cranberries: Christmas
  mincemeat and
  cranberry crumble
  bars 85
creeping crust cobbler 35
crème fraîche ice cream
  with blueberries and
  almond crumble 122–3
Croome, Worcs 49, 79
crumbles 8–27
custard 137–8
  proper egg custard 135

vanilla ice cream 136

devilled crab with
  Parmesan crumb
  topping 92–3
Dutch apple tart 50–1

Errdig, North Wales 49

fish with Cheddar and
  dill crumble 94–5
fruit cobblers 28–43
fruit crumbles 8–27

ginger: raspberry
  gingerbread crumble
  14
  vanilla ice cream with
  ginger crumble and
  rhubarb 120
gooseberries 62
  gooseberry custard
  crumble cake 60–1
  white chocolate and
  gooseberry crumble
  upside-down
  cheesecake 128–9
grunts 39
Gunby, Lincs 49

haddock and prawn
  cobbler 113
ham: turkey and ham
  cobbler 108–9
history: cobblers 112
  crumbles 83–4
honey ice cream with
  pears and pecan

crumble 124–5

ice cream: crème fraîche
  122–3
  honey 124–5
  vanilla 120, 136
Ickworth, Suffolk 79
Italian crumble cake
  63–4

Knightshayes, Devon 99

lamb: minced lamb with
  potato scone cobbler
  114–15
leek, Stilton and walnut
  crumble 97
lemon curd crumble
  muffins 70–1
Llanerchaeron, Wales 87
Lyveden,
  Northamptonshire 27

marzipan: quince, pear
  and apple crumble
  with marzipan 25–6
mincemeat: Christmas
  mincemeat and
  cranberry crumble
  bars 85
Moseley Old Hall, Staffs
  27
muffins 68–75
mug crumbles 130–2
mushrooms: chestnut
  and mushroom
  cobbler 104–5

Nostell Priory, West Yorks 121
Nunnington Hall, North Yorks 49

oranges: rhubarb and orange crumble tart 55–6

pandowdy 40–1
peaches 79
    fresh peach cobbler 31
    peach crumble cheesecake 126–7
pears 11, 54
    honey ice cream with pears and pecan crumble 124–5
    pear and hazelnut mug crumble 130
    pear cobbler 34
    quince, pear and apple crumble with marzipan 25–6
    toffee and pear crumble tart 52–3
Petworth, West Sussex 84
pistachios: apricot and pistachio crumble 21
plums 11, 79
    creeping crust cobbler 35
    plum and amaretti crumble 22
    plum crumble cake 57–8
potatoes: leek, Stilton and walnut crumble 97

minced lamb with potato scone cobbler 114–15
prawns: haddock and prawn cobbler 113
pumpkin 99
    spiced pumpkin muffins 72–3

quinces 27
    Italian crumble cake 63–4
    quince, pear and apple crumble with marzipan 25–6

raspberry gingerbread crumble 14
Red House, Bexleyheath, London 27
rhubarb 11, 121
    rhubarb and orange crumble tart 55–6
    rhubarb and strawberry crumble 13
    vanilla ice cream with ginger crumble and rhubarb 120

savoury cobblers 102–17
savoury crumbles 88–101
sbrisolona 63–5
Sizergh, Cumbria 27, 79
Slindon, Sussex 99
slumps 38, 39
soft fruit 87
sonkers 39
sour cream biscuits 42–3

spinach: fish with Cheddar and dill crumble 94–5
squash 99
strawberries: rhubarb and strawberry crumble 13
streusel 59, 74–5

tarts 50–6
Tatton Park, Cheshire 87, 99
toffee and pear crumble tart 52–3
tomatoes 99
    tomato and aubergine crumble 100–1
toppings: cobblers 33
    sweet crumbles 15–16
turkey and ham cobbler 108–9

vanilla ice cream 136
    with ginger crumble and rhubarb 120
vegetable cobbler 106
vegetables 99

Wimpole, Cambs 27, 79, 80, 87, 99
winter beef cobbler 110–11
Woolsthorpe Manor, Lincs 49

Zwetschgenkuchen 57–8

Acknowledgements

Thanks are due to many people: to Janalice Merry, Alison Mummery and Agnes Winter for help with recipes; to Stella Hobbs, Pamela Hartshorne, Will Johnson and Addy Johnson, all of whom relieved the household of excess crumble and made useful comments on the results; to Pearson's of Sinnington, soft fruit growers, who had gooseberries in the freezer when I needed some in January; at Pavilion, to Peter Taylor who commissioned the book, and Lucy Smith and Maggie Ramsay for careful editing. Most of all, thanks to my husband Derek Johnson, the person who is really the family crumble maker, but who nobly allowed me to experiment with the theme.